CONTROL
THE
PULSE

BREAK FREE FROM EMOTIONAL DECISIONS
AND DESIGN A LIFE THAT WORKS

TIERRE FORD

CONTROL THE PULSE

Copyright 2025 © By Tierre Ford

All rights reserved. No parts of this book may be reproduced or transmitted in any form or by any means electronic or mechanical without permission in writing from publisher

ABOUT THE AUTHOR

At just 12 years old, I started selling drugs in the 6th grade—following the blueprint I saw in my own home. My father was both a dealer and a user, and by the 7th grade, I had bought my first car, was paying my mama rent, and buying my own school clothes.

That same year, the school system labeled me as "slow." They placed me in a remedial reading class—embarrassed me, honestly. I was ashamed. But I still kept my swag, my gold chains, my Starter jackets, and my game face. I was one of the most popular kids in school, but truth be told, I had stopped learning. I was only there to show off.

Then one day, my reading teacher—who I'll never forget—looked me in my eyes and said, "You don't belong in this class. You're smart. Don't let them label you." Her words stuck with me, even though my CRT test scores said otherwise.

At age 12 years old I became my neighborhood's youngest drug supplier. I started with 10 dollars, and I flipped that all the way to over $500,000. Me and my Dad link up dealing together supplying the market. I dropped out of high school in the 10th grade. I bought my mother a house with a pool in the backyard, purchased luxury cars, before I was locked up at 19.

At that point in my life, I had never read a full book. Not one. But my father always told me, **"The mind is the most powerful tool in the universe. Street sense and book sense together? That's unstoppable."**

So I gave books a chance.

It started with street fiction. Then history. Then business. Then biographies about powerful and wealthy people. I started seeing myself in those pages—not always in their polish, but in their

CONTROL THE PULSE

ambition, their boldness. Then I read **Think and Grow Rich and As a Man Thinketh.** Those two books changed my entire mindset.

That's when I met my friend Cool Harris. I saw some of his writing on a notepad, and it rocked my world. I realized I had something to say, too. From that moment on, I picked up the pencil—and I've never looked back.

I earned my GED, took business and college courses, and started studying resilience. I discovered that, back in the day, Black people were once forbidden to read. There's even a saying: **"If you want to hide something from a Black person, put it in a book."** That became my fuel.

Now, I write both fiction and self-help books, covering everything from mindset and mental toughness to financial strategy and spiritual growth. I pour my soul into every page with one mission: to light a fire inside someone who's ready for change.

To everyone who's followed my journey—thank you. Let's set the world on fire with truth, with courage, with knowledge. Let's break every chain and every myth that says we don't read.

Peace—And Keep The Faith.

TIERRE FORD

SYNOPSIS

Your feelings aren't facts.
And your future depends on knowing the difference.

In a time where people are told to "feel everything," *Control the Pulse* dares to teach the opposite: how to think clearly, act with discipline, and build a life rooted in calm—not chaos.

Whether you're drowning in debt, stuck in toxic relationships, or just tired of starting over—this book gives you the mental playbook to stop reacting and start leading.

Inside you'll learn how to:

- Stop making emotional financial choices that sabotage your wealth
- Navigate love with logic, not lust or fear
- Build discipline in your health without hype or guilt
- Stay calm in high-pressure moments when others fold
- Replace motivation with mastery—and create real peace

This isn't therapy. This is strategy.
 Because emotional control isn't cold—it's powerful.

If you're ready to master your reactions, move with precision, and finally design a life that works—it's time to Control the Pulse.

CONTROL THE PULSE

TABLE OF CONTENTS

Copyright _____ II

Synopsis _____ III

Introduction _____ IX

1. Why Emotions Fail Us _____ 1
2. Feelings Vs. Facts: Learning The Difference _____ 4
3. The Cost Of Emotional Spending _____ 10
4. Heart Over Head — Relationship Regrets _____ 16
5. When Emotions Undermine Your Health _____ 22
6. How To Spot Emotional Bias In Real Time _____ 28
7. The Hidden Cost Of Impulse _____ 34
8. Emotional Triggers That Sabotage Your Goals _____ 39
9. Regret, Guilt & Revenge — The Silent Decision-Makers _____ 45
10. Who Profits From Your Emotional Reactions? _____ 51
11. Emotional Intelligence Vs. Emotional Control _____ 57
12. Reframing — Change The Meaning, Change The Outcome _____ 62
13. The Power Of Pause — Mastering Stillness Before Action _____ 67
14. Reframing — Change The Meaning, Change The Outcome _____ 72
15. Becoming The Ceo Of Your Life _____ 77
16. Replacing Emotion With Frameworks _____ 82
17. Detach, Don't Disconnect _____ 88

CONTROL THE PULSE

18. Mental Models Of Billionaires — Thinking Bigger Than Emotion ___93
19. Training Your Brain To Think In Outcomes, Not Reactions ___99
20. Understanding Delayed Gratification — Playing Long To Win Strong ___105
21. Emotional Spending Vs. Strategic Investing ___111
22. Learning The Language Of Logic — Speaking Truth Over Triggers ___117
23. Budgeting Without The Shame Spiral ___123
24. How Rich People Use Numbers, Not Nerves ___128
25. The Art Of Walking Away From A Bad Deal ___133
26. From Hustle To Discipline: Building True Wealth ___138
27. Money Arguments: Why Couples Fight & How To Stop ___142
28. Spending To Impress Is Emotionally Expensive ___147
29. Your Bank Account Doesn't Love You Back ___151
30. Get Rich Slow: The Emotionless Wealth Plan ___155
31. Attraction Vs. Alignment ___159
32. How To Date Without Losing Your Mind ___163
33. Lust, Love & Lies – Emotional Filters In Romance ___167
34. Attachment Styles And Financial Ruin ___171
35. Are You Choosing Or Escaping? ___176
36. High-Value Love Requires High-Value Thinking ___180
37. Standards Over Emotions In Relationships ___184

38. Arguing With Logic — How To Fight Fair _____ 188
39. Walking Away With Dignity, Not Drama _____ 193
40. Don't Build A Life With Someone Who Spends Emotionally _____ 197
41. Don't Let Comfort Kill You _____ 201
42. Emotional Eating, Lazy Thinking _____ 206
43. Cutting Toxic People Without Guilt _____ 211
44. Motivation Is Overrated—Discipline Wins _____ 215
45. How To Make Data-Driven Health Choices _____ 219
46. Why Mental Health Requires Mental Work _____ 224
47. Feel Good? Doesn't Mean It's Good For You _____ 228
48. Stop Justifying Your Vices _____ 233
49. Investing In Health Like It's A Business _____ 237
50. Becoming The Calm In Every Storm _____ 241

CONTROL THE PULSE

INTRODUCTION

"The Best Decisions You'll Ever Make… Will Have Nothing to Do With Emotion."

You've been taught to "follow your heart."

To "trust your gut."

To "do what feels right."

But what if I told you that the best version of your life—the wealth, love, and health you truly want—comes when you don't follow feelings first?

Emotions are real.

But they're not always reliable.

They'll make you chase approval, overspend to impress, stay in relationships you've outgrown, or avoid making the hard decisions that lead to real growth.

This book is not about becoming cold.

It's about becoming clear.

It's about learning to separate emotion from execution.

To pause before acting.

To observe before investing.

To love without losing yourself.

To choose discipline over dopamine.

The goal isn't to kill your feelings—it's to master them.

So you can finally make moves that serve you.

Welcome to the life you've been avoiding because it didn't feel good.

Now let's build the one that actually works.

CONTROL THE PULSE

CHAPTER 1

WHY EMOTIONS FAIL US

The Truth?

Most of the worst decisions you've made started with a feeling.

Think about it:

The thing you bought that you couldn't afford? That was emotion.

The text you sent late at night? Emotion.

The argument that spiraled into a breakup or fallout? Emotion.

Skipping the gym? Emotional comfort.

Staying silent when you should've spoken up? Emotional fear.

We are not broken because we feel.

We are broken because we let feelings run the show.

Emotions are fast. Loud. Reactive.

They tell us we need something now, or we'll lose it forever.

They make us think we're in love after three dates, or believe we're broke after one overdraft.

But emotions lie.

They exaggerate. They inflate. They dramatize.

And if you don't challenge them, they'll cost you everything.

The Pattern of Emotional Decisions Looks Like This:

CONTROL THE PULSE

1. A trigger hits (stress, boredom, desire, rejection).
2. The brain floods with chemicals—adrenaline, cortisol, dopamine.
3. You react: spend, yell, ghost, chase, quit, eat, scroll, ignore.
4. You regret it later.

We call it a "bad habit." But it's deeper. It's a bad response cycle.

And the only way to break it is to stop worshipping how you feel.

Want wealth? You can't spend emotionally.

Want love? You can't choose just based on chemistry.

Want health? You can't eat based on cravings.

This is the chapter where we get honest.

How many years have emotions cost you?

Look back.

That relationship you stayed in too long?

That money you blew trying to impress somebody?

That opportunity you passed on because you were scared?

That apology you never gave because of pride?

Those were feelings—not facts.

And once you understand that feelings are just internal weather—passing storms, not permanent states—you'll stop letting them run your life.

You're not weak. You're just wired for survival.

But survival is not the goal anymore.

Strategy is.

This book is the manual your parents didn't give you.

CONTROL THE PULSE

Not because they didn't love you—but because they were emotional too.

Starting today, we're going to slow down, zoom out, and make room for wisdom.

Emotions are passengers.

You are the driver.

It's time you took the wheel.

CHAPTER 2

FEELINGS VS. FACTS: LEARNING THE DIFFERENCE

"Feelings Are Not Facts. They're Signals. Learn To Read Them—But Don't Let Them Lead." — *Tierre Ford*

Let's Get Something Straight.

Just because it *feels* real, doesn't mean it *is*.

This is one of the hardest truths to accept, especially when the emotions come heavy. Anxiety. Lust. Rage. Loneliness. Fear. Love.

They arrive like hurricanes—loud, sweeping, convincing. They make you think what you're feeling is the full truth.

But it's not.
It's only *your* truth at that moment. Not *the* truth. And definitely not the whole truth.

The difference between people who build real wealth, stable love, and lasting health—and those who keep cycling through chaos—is this:

They've learned to separate how they feel from what is real.

STORY 1: THE CHECKING ACCOUNT THAT LIED

Marcus was 24 when he got his first real job. $65,000 a year. Felt like a million.

CONTROL THE PULSE

Two paychecks in, he bought a car off the lot. Not used. Not smart. New.

He called his mom from the dealership. "I deserve this," he said.

By the end of the year, he had $9,000 in credit card debt, three maxed-out store cards, and no savings.

But the payments were still coming in, so he *felt* fine.

Then he got laid off.

Two months later, the car was gone, the rent was late, and Marcus sat in a bar telling his friend: "Man, I don't know what happened. I felt like I was doing good."

That's the trap.
He *felt* wealthy—but the *facts* said otherwise.
He *felt* in control—but he never was.

FEELINGS ARE SHORT-TERM. FACTS ARE LONG-TERM.

Feelings change with sleep, weather, hormones, music, food, or a text message.

 Facts remain consistent regardless of your mood.

Here's how it plays out in real life:

- *Feeling:* "I think she's the one."
  Fact: You've known her for 3 weeks, and she hasn't told you her last name.

- *Feeling:* "I'm broke."
  Fact: You have $4,200 in savings but just had a slow month.

- *Feeling:* "I'm failing."
  Fact: You're tired. You need rest, not panic.

The emotional brain is wired for *now*.
The rational brain is wired for *patterns*.

CONTROL THE PULSE

If you only trust your feelings, you'll always need to *feel better* to act better.
But if you anchor to facts, you act smarter even when you don't feel like it.

STORY 2: THE TEXT THAT ALMOST ENDED A MARRIAGE

Angela and Tyrone had been married seven years.

One night, Tyrone stayed out later than usual. Didn't call.
Angela's mind ran wild.

"He's cheating."
"He's hiding something."
"I *knew* it. I *felt* it."

By the time he walked through the door, her emotions were boiling. He said, "Sorry baby, my phone died—I stopped by my brother's house. He just got out of the hospital."

But she didn't want the truth.
She wanted a *fight*.

That night turned into a shouting match. Three days of silence.
All because of *feelings*.
She never checked the facts. She just let her emotions be judged and jury.

Later, she admitted:
"My fear talks louder than logic."

And she's not alone.
Most people confuse insecurity with instinct.
Fear with facts.
Trauma with truth.

HOW TO PRACTICE FACT-FIRST THINKING

Here's a simple model to train your mind:

CONTROL THE PULSE

The 3 R's of Rational Decision-Making:

1. **Recognize** the feeling
   Pause and name it: "I feel anxious." "I feel rejected." "I feel excited."

2. **Review** the facts
   Ask:
   - What actually happened?
   - What do I *know*, not just suspect?
   - What else could be true?

3. **Respond** based on facts—not feelings
   Act with clarity. Speak with calm. Move with evidence.

FEELINGS ARE DATA—NOT DECISIONS

Think of emotions like dashboard warning lights.
They tell you *something* is happening—but not *everything*.

- Anger may mean a boundary was crossed.
- Fear may mean something matters.
- Sadness may mean it's time to let go.
- Loneliness may mean you need connection—not validation.

But those are invitations to *reflect*, not commands to *react*.

Smart people don't ignore feelings.
They just don't obey them blindly.

STORY 3: WHEN FEELING "READY" NEVER COMES

Jason wanted to launch his business. He had the plan, the skills, and the time.
But every time he sat down to start, a voice whispered:
"You're not ready."

CONTROL THE PULSE

"You might fail."
"What if nobody buys?"

So he waited. And waited.
Two years passed.
He watched three other people launch similar businesses and take off.

Eventually, he realized:
"I was waiting for confidence. But confidence comes *after* action—not before it."

The *feeling* of readiness never showed up.
But the *facts* were always there: He was qualified. He was prepared.

He was just scared.
And that fear cost him momentum.

IN LOVE, MONEY, AND HEALTH—FEELINGS FOOL PEOPLE EVERY DAY

- People fall in love with a fantasy, not the facts.
- They spend money because they're bored, not because they need something.
- They skip workouts because they don't feel like it, not because they're incapable.

The truth is, most of what's holding you back isn't your situation. It's your *reaction* to it.

And the moment you slow down and ask,
"What are the *facts* right now?"
You start to take your power back.

LET THIS BE YOUR NEW DEFAULT:

Before you buy—check your numbers.
Before you commit—check the consistency.

CONTROL THE PULSE

Before you react—check your patterns.
Before you judge—check the full story.
Before you quit—check the scoreboard.

And most of all...

Before you say, *"I feel like..."*
Ask: *"But what do I know?"*

Because feelings are valid—but they are not always valuable.

Narrator's Reflection:

You don't have to be emotionless.
You just have to be emotionally **wise**.

It's not about silencing your feelings.
It's about stacking them next to facts—and choosing based on what leads to progress, not what feeds your pain.

This is how wealth is protected.
This is how love matures.
This is how health is sustained.

The moment you learn to pause... and question the story your feelings are telling...
You stop reacting like a victim —and start responding like a leader.

CONTROL THE PULSE

CHAPTER 3

THE COST OF EMOTIONAL SPENDING

"Every Dollar You Spend Emotionally Is A Seed You Steal From Your Future Self." — *Tierre Ford*

Some people don't need enemies.
They've got impulse.

Swipe now. Regret later.
Spend now. Stress later.
Buy now. Blame the world later.

If money could talk, it would say one thing loud and clear:
"I don't solve emotional problems. I just expose them."

We all want financial freedom.
But the question is—how many of us are emotionally *mature* enough to handle it?

The truth is:
Most people are broke not because they don't make money—but because they *spend emotionally*.

STORY 1: THE LOUIS BAG THAT ATE HER LIGHT BILL

Bri was making just enough.

She had rent, a car note, daycare, and a job she didn't love.
But tax season hit. She got her refund—$4,600. It felt like a new beginning.

CONTROL THE PULSE

So she bought a Louis Vuitton bag.
On sale, she told herself. Justified it as a gift to herself. "I've been through a lot," she said.

Three weeks later, her light bill hit. Her balance was short.
The bag sat on the couch looking beautiful—but couldn't keep the lights on.

What she didn't realize was this:
The bag didn't fix her pain. It dressed it up.

THE TRUTH ABOUT EMOTIONAL SPENDING

You don't just spend money when you need something.
You spend money when you're trying to *feel* something.

- Lonely? You shop.
- Sad? You eat out.
- Bored? You scroll Amazon.
- Heartbroken? You book a flight.
- Insecure? You flex online.

This is how society profits:
By convincing you that healing comes in a box, or a label, or a brand.
It doesn't. It never has.

Emotional spending is self-medication with receipts.
And the interest rate is painful.

STORY 2: THE $500 NIGHT OUT THAT COST HIM 5 YEARS

Derrick had just gotten promoted.
He was 30, had a clean apartment, a nice car, and no savings.

His friend said, "Bro, you worked hard. Let's celebrate big."

CONTROL THE PULSE

So they hit the club. Bottle service. VIP. Designer shoes he couldn't afford.
One night: $500 gone.

Two weeks later, his car broke down. Needed $600.
He didn't have it.
Had to take out a payday loan—$600 at 35% interest.

That $500 night turned into a 5-year debt spiral.

Because the *celebration* felt good,
But the *discipline* would've felt better.

EMOTIONAL SPENDING IS A REACTION TO AN INNER VOID

Ask yourself this:

What are you really buying when you spend emotionally?

- Approval?
- Attention?
- Status?
- Comfort?
- Distraction?

Because **if the problem is emotional, the solution is never financial.**

You're not "treating yourself."
You're avoiding yourself.

And the companies you buy from? They know it.
They design ads to trigger feelings. Urgency. Scarcity. FOMO.

They don't sell clothes.
They sell *confidence*.
They don't sell meals.
They sell *belongings*.

CONTROL THE PULSE

They don't sell cars.
They sell *power*.

But none of it lasts.
Because if you need a purchase to feel whole, you'll always need another one.

WHAT YOU'RE REALLY PAYING FOR

Here's what emotional spending really costs you:

- **Time** — You delay goals trying to catch up.
- **Peace** — You lose sleep over balances and bills.
- **Freedom** — You can't move how you want when debt owns your choices.
- **Growth** — You keep solving grown-up problems with childish thinking.

And worst of all?
You're building a future you don't even like, just to feel better today.

THE FEELING FADES. THE PAYMENT STAYS.

Let's be honest:

- That $300 outfit you wore once? Can't return it.
- That $1,200 vacation? The pictures were great. The bill is greater.
- That $15 lunch every day? It's adding up to $450/month. That's a car note.

None of this makes you a bad person.
But it does make you *vulnerable*.

Because every dollar you spend without purpose...
Is a dollar your future self will have to explain or repay.

CONTROL THE PULSE

STORY 3: THE MAN WHO SAVED $50K BY GETTING THERAPY

Jermaine used to call himself a "high roller."
Always had the newest kicks, popped bottles every Friday, posted his wristwatch like a brand.

But underneath the flash was grief.
His dad died when he was 19. His mom battled depression.
Spending made him feel alive. Important. Seen.

One day, his friend asked him:
"Have you ever tried *talking* to someone instead of *buying* your way through pain?"

He didn't like that question.
But it stuck.

Six months later, he started therapy.
In the first session, he cried. By session eight, he admitted:
"I was shopping to avoid myself."

Now?
He budgets. He invests. He runs a mentoring group for boys with father wounds.
And he's saved $50,000—more than he ever thought possible.

HOW TO STOP EMOTIONAL SPENDING BEFORE IT STARTS

Here's a three-part tool to shift your behavior:

1. PAUSE.
Before you swipe your card or hit "add to cart," stop and ask:

"What am I really trying to feel right now?"

2. PLAN.
Create a monthly "emotional budget."

CONTROL THE PULSE

Give yourself space for fun—but set limits.
Ex: "$200 for fun. Not $2,000 to feel better about a breakup."

3. PURPOSE.
Before big purchases, wait 48 hours.
If it still aligns with your goals and values—go for it.
If not? Let it pass.

YOU DESERVE NICE THINGS—BUT NOT AT THE EXPENSE OF YOUR FUTURE

This isn't about being cheap.
It's about being *clear*.

If you want wealth, you've got to stop trading your peace for a quick pleasure.
Stop dressing your trauma in designer.
Stop confusing spending with self-worth.

You are not what you buy.
You are what you build.
And you can't build anything strong on a foundation of feelings.

Narrator's Reflection:

You can love nice things without letting them define you.
You can enjoy life without spending to impress people who won't show up when you're broke.
You can look rich now—or be wealthy forever.

The emotional high is temporary.
The consequences are not.

The next time you feel the urge to spend, ask yourself one question:

"Is this helping me feel better—or helping me *get better*?"

One keeps you stuck.
The other sets you free.

CHAPTER 4

HEART OVER HEAD — RELATIONSHIP REGRETS

> "Love Is Not Blind. It's Just That Most People Close Their Eyes When It's Time To Walk Away." — *Tierre Ford*

There's a reason why some of your biggest regrets wear perfume.
Or cologne.
Or send late-night "you up?" texts.

Relationships are beautiful.
But emotional ones—unchecked, unbalanced, and unexamined—are dangerous.

Some of the most expensive decisions in life don't come from Wall Street.
They come from bedrooms.
And breakups.
And the six-month "situationship" that turned into six years of lost time.

Let's be clear:

Falling in love is easy.
Staying when you shouldn't is emotional.
Leaving when it's time is strategic.

STORY 1: THE SIX-YEAR SETBACK

Tonya met Jamal at 22.
He was charming, funny, and had big dreams.
At 28, she realized that "big dreams" had turned into "big excuses."

CONTROL THE PULSE

He hadn't held a steady job in three years.
She was working two jobs.
He said he was "figuring it out." She was covering rent and counseling him through every spiral.

Still, when her friends told her to leave, she said,
"But I love him."

Love.
The word that kept her stuck.
The emotion that made her ignore the facts.

When she finally left, she cried—not because she missed him, but because she realized she should've left *four years earlier.*

She wasn't in love.
She was in **fear**—of starting over.
She was in **guilt**—for wanting more.
She was in **hope**—that maybe he'd change.

That's not a relationship.
That's an emotional hostage situation.

LOVE WITHOUT LOGIC IS A LIABILITY

We've been sold fairy tales.
Movies. Music. Stories. Soulmates.
But nobody told us that healthy love comes with hard choices.

- Sometimes you outgrow people you still care about.
- Sometimes chemistry hides chaos.
- Sometimes your heart wants what your life *can't* afford.

Here's the truth:
The heart may lead you into love,
But it's your **mind** that determines if you stay.

CONTROL THE PULSE

EMOTIONAL RELATIONSHIPS LEAD TO LOGICAL CONSEQUENCES

Think about it:
- How many times did you go back to someone you knew wasn't right for you?
- How many hours did you lose re-reading old messages, hoping for a sign?
- How many tears have you cried over people who wouldn't even answer a phone call now?

That's not love. That's *attachment*.
That's emotional entrapment—when your head knows the truth, but your heart keeps rewriting it.

STORY 2: MARRIED TO POTENTIAL

Carlos was stable. Vanessa was exciting.
He loved her energy. Her fire. Her confidence.

But every six months, there was a new "career shift."
A new fallout with friends. A new breakdown.
And Carlos became the emotional janitor—always cleaning up behind her chaos.

He told himself,
"She just needs time."
"She's been through a lot."
"She's growing."

But the truth was:
She wasn't growing.
She was spinning.
And Carlos was the one getting dizzy.
Three years in, he realized:
He didn't love *her*. He loved her *potential*.
And he was sacrificing his peace to keep a possibility alive.

CONTROL THE PULSE

RED FLAGS ARE NOT PROJECTS—THEY'RE WARNINGS

Stop trying to fix what's not yours.
You are not a rehab center.
You are not a therapist.
You are not a messiah.

Loving someone doesn't mean staying past the expiration date.
Forgiving doesn't mean repeating.
Understanding doesn't mean accepting.

Your heart may want to heal them.
But your mind has to protect *you*.

THE REGRET NO ONE TALKS ABOUT

Most people think regret comes from who they *lost*.
But often, the deepest regret is who you became trying to keep them.

- The version of you that stopped laughing.
- The version that stopped dreaming.
- The one that tolerated things you once said you'd never accept.

And when the relationship finally end?
You don't just grieve for the person.
You grieve the *you* you lost along the way.

HEAD OVER HEART: HOW TO LOVE SMARTER

Loving logically doesn't mean loving cold.
It means loving **with clarity.**

Here's how to start:

1. Set Standards, Not Just Feelings
Does this person align with your values, not just your vibe?

CONTROL THE PULSE

2. Ask: Is This Sustainable?
Good love doesn't drain you—it fuels you. Check the emotional budget.

3. Watch Patterns, Not Apologies
Everyone makes mistakes. But is there *growth*? Or just guilt manipulation?

4. Take Notes, Not Just Hints
If someone shows you who they are—*believe them the first time.*

5. Know the Difference Between History and Harmony
Just because you've been through a lot with someone doesn't mean they're right for your future.

STORY 3: THE ONE WHO CHOSE HERSELF

Sasha was engaged at 31.

Everything looked perfect on paper.
Nice guy. Good career. Big wedding planned.

But in her gut, something always felt... off.

He didn't listen.
He interrupted her ideas.
He made jokes that stung, then laughed it off like she was "too sensitive."

She started therapy.
And her therapist asked one question:

"Would you want your daughter to marry someone like him?"

She sat in silence.
That silence held the answer.

Two months later, she called it off.
People called her crazy. Said she'd regret it.

CONTROL THE PULSE

But years later, she's married to someone who respects her voice, not just her looks.

And she says,
"The best decision I ever made was *leaving something good-looking for something good-hearted.*"

Narrator's Reflection:

We all want love.
But when you let your heart lead without guidance, you'll walk into traps smiling—because it *feels right.*

Real love doesn't blur your mind. It clears it.
It aligns with your purpose.
It protects your peace.
It doesn't require you to shrink, settle, or suffer.

The next time you feel pulled into something chaotic, ask yourself:

"Is this love… or just emotional survival dressed up in romance?"

Because peace is more attractive than passion that burns you.
And the smartest love decisions are made

CONTROL THE PULSE

CHAPTER 5

WHEN EMOTIONS UNDERMINE YOUR HEALTH

"Your Body Listens To What Your Mind Believes—Even When It's Lying To You." — *Tierre Ford*

Your health doesn't start in the gym.
It starts in your *mind*.

That's where decisions are made.
Where cravings are justified.
Where excuses are born.
Where guilt and shame live like squatters.

You can eat kale, drink water, and still destroy your health—if your thoughts are toxic.
Because the truth is, **most health issues don't start on your plate. They start in your patterns.**

And most patterns are emotional.

STORY 1: THE BURGER THAT BROKE HER PROMISE

Jasmine had been eating clean for six weeks.
No fast food. Drinking more water. Walking every day. Feeling better.

Then her boyfriend ghosted her after an argument.
That night, she ordered two burgers, fries, ice cream, and soda.
"I deserved it," she said.

But she wasn't eating for fuel. She was eating for *comfort*.
By morning, her stomach hurt.
By evening, her confidence did.

CONTROL THE PULSE

It wasn't the food that broke her.
It was the emotion she fed—without thinking.

EMOTIONAL HEALTH HABITS AREN'T JUST PHYSICAL— THEY'RE PSYCHOLOGICAL

Here's how emotions start breaking your health:

- **Stress says**: "You're too tired to cook."
- **Guilt says**: "You already messed up. Might as well finish the cake."
- **Anxiety says**: "Eat now—you'll feel better."
- **Depression says**: "Don't move. Sleep. Hide. Wait."
- **Shame says**: "You'll always be like this. Why try?"

That voice isn't your body.
That's your mind—**trying to regulate emotion with the wrong tools.**

THE SILENT DAMAGE OF STRESS

You don't need to get shot to be dying.
Some people are being killed slowly by stress—quiet, invisible, daily.

Chronic stress leads to:

- Hormone imbalance
- Inflammation
- Sleep disorders
- Blood pressure spikes
- Immune system shutdown

And all of that is emotional.
You're not weak.

CONTROL THE PULSE

You're overwhelmed.
But the cost is the same.

Stress doesn't just weigh on your mind—it wears out your body.

STORY 2: THE MAN WHO SLEPT HIS SUCCESS AWAY

Kevin was a high-performing real estate agent.
Always working. Always hustling. Always available.

But he wasn't sleeping.

He told himself: "I'll rest when I'm rich."
Four hours a night. Coffee all day. Go-mode.

Then one morning, he passed out at a showing.
Tests revealed adrenal fatigue, a weakened heart, and severe dehydration.

He wasn't a bad businessman.
He was a **burnt-out** one.
Running on stress.
Performing for validation.
And feeding the lie that *success requires self-destruction*.

IF YOUR HEALTH ISN'T EMOTIONAL, WHY IS IT SO HARD TO STAY CONSISTENT?

We all know what to do.

- Eat better.
- Move more.
- Sleep well.
- Stay hydrated.
- Manage stress.

CONTROL THE PULSE

But knowing isn't the problem.
Feeling is.

You know how to cook—but you feel too tired.
You know how to stretch—but you feel too overwhelmed.
You know that soda isn't helping—but it makes you feel in control.

So the question becomes:

Are you treating your body like a temple?
Or like a temporary escape route for your feelings?

HEALTH IS BUILT ON DISCIPLINE—NOT MOTIVATION

Motivation depends on mood.
Discipline depends on *commitment*.

Discipline says: "I work out whether I feel like it or not."
Discipline says: "I drink water even when I want juice."
Discipline says: "I honor my future, not just my frustration."

That's the difference between a goal and a lifestyle.

STORY 3: THE WOMAN WHO WALKED OFF HER TRAUMA

Marissa had gained 40 pounds in two years.
It started after a bad breakup and two deaths in her family.

She tried diets. She tried boot camps. But she kept quitting.

Then one day, her therapist told her:
"Walk. Not to lose weight. But to release pain."

So she walked.
Every day.
No music. No scale. Just herself, her thoughts, and the road.

Six months later, she'd lost the weight.
But more importantly—she'd *reclaimed her power.*

She said,
"I stopped trying to shrink my body and started trying to release

CONTROL THE PULSE

my grief.
And health followed."

EMOTIONAL SELF-CARE IS PHYSICAL CARE

Here's how to start protecting your health from your emotions:

1. Name the Feeling

"I'm not hungry. I'm sad."
"I'm not tired. I'm avoiding."
"I'm not lazy. I'm overwhelmed."

2. Choose a Better Outlet

Instead of eating, can you go for a walk?
Instead of scrolling, can you stretch or journal?

3. Create Rituals, Not Reactions

Build routines that protect your peace *before* stress comes.
Schedule rest. Plan meals. Set boundaries. Take walks. Say "no."

4. Stop Shaming Yourself Into Change

You don't hate your way into healing.
You respect yourself there.

YOUR HEALTH IS A LOVE LETTER TO YOUR FUTURE SELF

You can't take your goals seriously and keep abusing your body.
You can't talk about elevation while feeding addiction.
You can't want peace but refuse to sleep.
You can't ask for strength but avoid movement.

Your body is the one place you have to live in for the rest of your life.

Treat it like home.
Not a landfill for stress, grief, or neglect.

Narrator's Reflection:

CONTROL THE PULSE

Your health isn't just about calories and workouts.
It's about choosing *wholeness* over chaos.
It's about honoring your body the same way you want to be honored in relationships or business.

Because emotional pain ignored will always find a physical outlet.
And the cure won't come from another diet.
It'll come from stillness.
From discipline.
From choosing clarity over comfort—again and again.

Next time your emotions tell you to rest, eat, escape, or quit—pause.
Ask yourself:

"Is this healing me—or hiding me?"

Because you deserve a body that thrives.
Not just survives the aftermath of your feelings.

CONTROL THE PULSE

CHAPTER 6

HOW TO SPOT EMOTIONAL BIAS IN REAL TIME

"If You Don't Slow Down And Question Your Emotions, They'll Convince You To Repeat Every Mistake You Swore You'd Never Make Again." — *Tierre Ford*

You already know how it goes:

- "It just felt right."
- "I didn't even think about it—I just did it."
- "I knew better, but something came over me."

That *something* is emotional bias.

It's not random.
It's not harmless.
It's a blindfold.

Emotional bias is the quiet lie your brain tells you to justify decisions that serve your feelings—not your future.

And the worst part?
You don't see it *while it's happening.*
You only recognize it once the damage is done.

This chapter is about flipping that.
Catching the lie *while it's speaking.*

STORY 1: THE BUSINESS DEAL THAT LOOKED LIKE DESTINY

James had always wanted to open a clothing store.

CONTROL THE PULSE

When his cousin came to him with a "perfect opportunity"—cheap space, a plug on inventory, and a "can't-miss" pop-up—James jumped in.
No contract. No lawyer. No second thought.

"It felt like the sign I'd been waiting for," he said.

Two months in, the cousin disappeared.
The lease was never in James's name.
And $6,000 worth of inventory vanished overnight.

What went wrong?

He made a permanent move off a temporary feeling.
He didn't check the math. He chased the mood.

WHAT IS EMOTIONAL BIAS?

It's when your brain uses feelings as facts—*especially* under pressure.

You'll see it when you:

- Choose comfort over clarity
- Pick loyalty over logic
- React based on fear instead of strategy
- Ignore red flags because "it just feels right"
- Justify the same behavior you'd judge in someone else

And if you don't spot it early, it *runs* your life behind the scenes.

THE MOST COMMON EMOTIONAL BIASES

1. Confirmation Bias

You believe what *feels familiar.* You ignore what challenges your emotions.

CONTROL THE PULSE

"See? I knew he was still thinking about me. He liked my story."
(But didn't respond to your message.)

2. Loss Aversion Bias

You stay in bad situations because you fear losing what you already invested.

"I can't leave this job now—I've been here five years."
(Even though it's draining your health.)

3. Halo Bias

You excuse someone's toxic traits because they're attractive, talented, or have history with you.

"Yeah, she lied again—but she's been through a lot."
(So have you.)

4. Anchoring Bias

You base your decision on the first offer or idea—even when new data shows better options.

"I've always done it this way."
(Even though 'this way' has kept you broke.)

STORY 2: THE FRIEND WHO COULDN'T BE TOLD

Nicole was in love with a man who loved everyone but her.
He came around when he wanted. Disappeared when he didn't.
But when her friends confronted her, she said,
"You don't know him like I do."

That's emotional bias in full effect.

She wasn't defending *him*.
She was defending her *attachment to the version of him she made up*.

And that's what emotional bias does—it convinces you to stay loyal to a fantasy while reality burns behind you.

CONTROL THE PULSE

HOW TO CATCH EMOTIONAL BIAS IN THE MOMENT

Here's a 4-question checkpoint to run any decision through:

1. "What am I feeling right now?"
Identify the emotion. Name it so it can't sneak past you.

2. "What's the data saying—not my drama?"
Look at the facts. Track records. Outcomes. Evidence.

3. "Would I advise a loved one to do this?"
If you'd tell your sibling, best friend, or child to walk away—why are you still there?

4. "If I delayed this by 48 hours, would I still want it?"
Emotional bias thrives in urgency. Time exposes the truth.

STORY 3: THE MAN WHO TRADED HIS PEACE FOR PRIDE

Aaron had a chance to make peace with his brother after years of fighting.

The call was made. The door was open.

But his pride said,
"They need to apologize first."

He waited.

That was five years ago.
His brother passed away unexpectedly last winter.
And Aaron's words at the funeral were,
"I thought we had more time."

Pride *felt* right in the moment.
But it cost him a lifetime of healing.

EMOTIONAL BIAS FEELS GOOD NOW—BUT COSTS MORE LATER

It's the "yes" you didn't mean.
The "no" you wish you could take back.

CONTROL THE PULSE

The silence you gave when you should've spoken.
The energy you wasted trying to prove something.

All of it?
Emotional bias.

It doesn't care about your future.
It cares about your comfort.
It wants you to act *now*, not think *through*.

BUILDING EMOTIONAL CLARITY

Here's how to train your mind:

- **Start journaling decisions.** Write what you're feeling and what you're doing. Patterns will appear.
- **Get outside perspective.** Someone not emotionally involved sees what you don't.
- **Practice delay.** Give everything that feels urgent at least 24 hours—especially texts, purchases, and deals.
- **Say out loud what you're believing.** If it sounds irrational, it probably is.

"If I don't say yes to this offer now, I'll miss my one shot."
(False. Emotionally biased. You're acting from scarcity.)

"I need to stay with them because they need me."
(Are you helping them heal—or enabling their harm?)

Narrator's Reflection:

Emotional bias doesn't scream. It whispers.
It sits quietly in your thoughts, shaping what you see, who you trust, and how you choose.

But once you see it, you *can't unsee it.*
You'll hear the lie *while* it's forming.

CONTROL THE PULSE

And you'll start making decisions that look like wisdom—not desperation.

Next time you feel the pressure to react fast, remember:

"Just because it feels familiar, doesn't mean it's right."

"Just because it feels good, doesn't mean it's safe."

"Just because it feels urgent, doesn't mean it's real."

Slow it down.
Catch the lie.
Move with logic—even when your emotions are loud.

CHAPTER 7

THE HIDDEN COST OF IMPULSE

"Impulse Is Expensive. It Never Shows You The Receipt Until It's Too Late." — *Tierre Ford*

You didn't plan to mess up.
You didn't schedule a setback.
It just *happened.*

One click. One call. One drink. One kiss. One swipe. One "just this once."

That's how most people lose.

Not through destruction—through **impulse.**
Not a bomb… but a slow, silent leak.
Tiny decisions that *feel* harmless but **compound** into chaos.

The truth?
Impulse is the enemy of legacy.

STORY 1: THE SNAP DECISION THAT COST HER A YEAR

Maya was frustrated.
Work stress. Family drama. Rent overdue.

She opened her laptop and searched for flights.
Clicked "Book Now" to Puerto Rico. $670 on her credit card. "I need this," she told herself.

She posted beach photos, sipping drinks and writing captions like "self-care" and "mental reset."

CONTROL THE PULSE

But when she got home, her lights were off.
Her landlord had changed the locks.
The $670 vacation turned into a $2,800 eviction—late fees, moving costs, and storage.

The trip *felt* like freedom.
But the **impulse stole her stability.**

WHAT IS IMPULSE, REALLY?

Impulse is emotional pressure pretending to be urgency.
It says:

- "Now or never."
- "You deserve this."
- "Just one time."
- "You'll figure it out later."

And it *always* leaves you with the worst part—**later.**

THE SCIENCE BEHIND IMPULSE

Your brain has two primary systems:

- **System 1:** Fast, emotional, reactive.
- **System 2:** Slow, logical, strategic.

Impulse lives in System 1.
It doesn't check the budget.
It doesn't read the contract.
It doesn't care about the consequences.

It just *acts.*

And every time you let impulse lead, System 2 gets weaker.
You start *trusting* the voice that got you in trouble.

CONTROL THE PULSE

STORY 2: THE TEXT THAT CHANGED EVERYTHING

Andre had moved on. He really had.

New girl. New job. New mindset.
But one night, lonely and scrolling, he saw his ex post a throwback.
They'd been toxic. But the *feeling* returned.

He typed:
"Been thinking about you. Hope you good."

She responded.
That text turned into a call.
That call turned into one night.

And that night?
It turned into a broken new relationship. A lost job. And emotional spiral.

Why?

Impulse traded healing for history.

THE LIES IMPULSE TELLS YOU

1. **"This won't matter tomorrow."**
    → It will.
2. **"I can afford it."**
    → Can your *future* afford it?
3. **"I'm in control."**
    → Then why did you do what you swore you wouldn't?
4. **"I'll fix it later."**
    → Later always costs more.

Impulse isn't just about money.
It's about patterns.
And patterns become character.

HOW TO SPOT AN IMPULSE DECISION

Ask yourself:

CONTROL THE PULSE

- Am I trying to escape a feeling or solve a problem?
- Would I still choose this if nobody ever saw it?
- Am I rushing because I'm afraid to pause?
- Does this align with my *long-term* values—or just my *short-term* mood?

If you can't answer clearly—**you're not deciding. You're reacting.**

STORY 3: THE MAN WHO COUNTED THE COST

Derrick used to have a rule: "I don't look at price tags."

He loved the rush. Shoes. Jewelry. Bottles. Last-minute trips.
He called it "manifesting abundance."

Then one day his debit card declined at the pharmacy.
He had overdrafted by $2.17.

Standing in that line, holding his stomach meds,
he realized: **"I spent $1,200 this weekend and can't afford to breathe right now."**

That was the day he wrote on his bathroom mirror:
"Think. Then buy."

Six months later, he was debt-free.
Because he stopped buying into impulse and started building discipline.

TOOLS TO BEAT IMPULSE IN THE MOMENT

1. The 10-10-10 Rule
Ask:

How will I feel about this in 10 minutes?
10 days?
10 months?

2. Set Spending Limits with Emotion in Mind
Budget for spontaneous joy—so it doesn't become survival stress.

CONTROL THE PULSE

3. Have an Exit Plan for Triggers
Know what you'll do when bored, anxious, lonely, angry.
Impulse thrives in those windows.

4. Keep a Consequence Journal
Write down every impulsive decision you regret.
Keep that list close.

It's not to shame you.
It's to *remind* you.

WHAT IMPULSE REALLY STEALS

- Your money
- Your time
- Your peace
- Your relationships
- Your power

Impulse is a thief.
But the worst part is—you hand it the keys.

Narrator's Reflection:

Every time you act on impulse, you vote for a future that you'll have to clean up.
But every time you pause, breathe, and choose alignment over adrenaline—you build a life with less regret.

Next time the pressure builds and your hand's on the trigger—
remember this:

"If you can't afford to think about it,

you can't afford to do it."

Take the pause.
Count the cost.
And give yourself the future that impulse keeps trying to steal.

CONTROL THE PULSE

CHAPTER 8

EMOTIONAL TRIGGERS THAT SABOTAGE YOUR GOALS

"You're Not Lazy. You're Not Broken. You're Triggered. And If You Don't Face It, You'll Keep Calling Sabotage A Personality Trait." — *Tierre Ford*

You set the goal.
You made the vision board.
You wrote the affirmation.
You were locked in—until something small... *flipped your switch.*

That's the part nobody talks about.
The moment when the grind is going great—
and then *BOOM*: a text, a tone, a look, a memory, a sound, a setback—and suddenly you're spiraling.

That's not a coincidence. That's a **trigger.**

And if you don't recognize your emotional triggers, they'll keep hijacking your progress like clockwork.

STORY 1: THE CLIENT WHO GHOSTED HER FUTURE

Bria had finally gotten a coach.
She was writing her first e-book, committed to losing 15 pounds, and stacking money with discipline.
Then she got a call: her ex was engaged.

She hung up the phone and said out loud,
"Why do I even try?"

That night, she didn't write.
She ate whatever.

CONTROL THE PULSE

She spent $300 online.
And she texted someone she knew was no good for her.

Her trigger wasn't *the news*—
It was the old *belief* that she wasn't enough.

And that belief had been waiting… for the *right* moment to come take the wheel.

WHAT IS A TRIGGER?

A trigger is a **stimulus that awakens old emotion**—usually pain, rejection, failure, or abandonment.

It doesn't ask for permission.
It bypasses your logic and yanks you back to a version of you that feels powerless.

And when that version shows up—your goals get ghosted.

THE TOP 6 TRIGGERS THAT DERAIL SUCCESS

1. Rejection

One "no" and you start questioning your whole path.

"Maybe I'm not cut out for this…"

2. Comparison

Scrolling through wins that aren't yours can lead to shame-fueled quitting.

"They're ahead. I'm behind. What's the point?"

3. Impatience

You expect quick results. When they don't show? Self-sabotage.

"If this was meant to be, it would've worked by now."

4. Guilt

Success feels like you're leaving people behind.

CONTROL THE PULSE

"My family is struggling and I'm out here trying to thrive?"

5. Criticism

One negative comment outweighs ten wins.

"Maybe they're right. Who do I think I am?"

6. Old Trauma

A smell, a word, a tone—anything can spark a reaction from a wound you never healed.

STORY 2: THE MAN WHO QUIT BEFORE HE BEGAN

Marcus had a business idea. He pitched it at a small event.

One person said:

"I don't really get it. That sounds confusing."

He laughed it off in the moment. But inside? His teenage self—the one who always felt misunderstood—stood up.

That night, he deleted the business plan.
Didn't tell anybody.

Not because it wasn't good.
But because one comment pulled up a trigger named "You're too much, nobody gets you."

That *emotion* stole his *execution*.

TRIGGERS DON'T CARE ABOUT YOUR GOALS

They don't care about your timeline, your hard work, or your discipline.
They only care about survival.

Triggers are rooted in old emotional responses, not current truth.

And they don't always show up loud.
Sometimes, they whisper:

CONTROL THE PULSE

- "Take a break."
- "You don't need to do this today."
- "Just one scroll. Just one snack. Just one night off..."

And before you know it—
you've delayed your destiny for a dopamine hit.

HOW TO DEFUSE A TRIGGER BEFORE IT BLOWS

1. Name It In Real Time
Say it out loud.

"I feel rejected."
"This reminded me of when I felt invisible."
"I'm not quitting—I'm triggered."

Naming it gives you back power.

2. Use the Trigger to Reveal the Wound
Ask:

"Where have I felt this before?"
"What's this really about?"

Often, the trigger isn't about *now*.
It's about a past version of you crying out to be seen and healed.

3. Create a Reframe Script
Instead of letting the trigger take over, pre-write the truth.

"Even if I feel behind, I'm still growing."
"One person's 'no' doesn't cancel my 'yes.'"
"This feeling is familiar, but I'm not that person anymore."

4. Anchor Back to the Vision
Keep a visual or statement of your goal nearby.
When the trigger hits, *touch your truth.*

CONTROL THE PULSE

STORY 3: THE WOMAN WHO STOPPED RUNNING FROM HER TRIGGERS

Alondra used to quit every time things got hard.

She'd ghost jobs, block men, cancel goals, binge-watch shows—then call it "needing space."

In therapy, her breakthrough came with one question:

"What are you trying not to feel when you disappear?"

That hit was different.

She realized her trigger wasn't laziness—it was **fear of disappointment.**
So she'd rather walk away than fail.

Now? She tracks her triggers.
When the urge to run hits, she breathes. Writes. Re-centers.
And finishes what she starts.

Not because it got easier—
But because she finally stopped letting pain drive her plans.

Narrator's Reflection:

Your goals are real.
Your vision is valid.
But if you don't confront your triggers, you'll keep finding new ways to sabotage the very future you're working toward.

Triggers are not stop signs.
They are signals—alerts that part of your past still needs attention.

But they don't get to decide how your story ends.

Next time your body wants to shut down, your mind wants to quit, or your habits want to repeat—pause.

CONTROL THE PULSE

Ask:

"Is this the truth?
Or is this a wound pretending to protect me?"

Then choose the version of you that's *healing*, not the one that's hiding.

CHAPTER 9

REGRET, GUILT & REVENGE — THE SILENT DECISION-MAKERS

"Some People Don't Move Forward Because They're Waiting For Pain To Approve It. Others Only Move Out Of Guilt Or To Prove Something. Either Way—You're Still Not Free."
— *Tierre Ford*

You can't always see it.
But something is guiding the wheel.

Not your vision.
Not your plan.
Not even your values.

It's an invisible force—a weight in your chest, a knot in your stomach, a fire in your jaw.
It's called **regret. Guilt. Revenge.**

And if you don't name it, it will name every decision you make.

STORY 1: THE BUSINESS BUILT ON PROVING THEM WRONG

Trey didn't start his company for freedom.
He started it because his ex said,
"You'll never be more than a delivery driver."

So he built.
Posted.
Flexed.

CONTROL THE PULSE

Made money.
Made moves.

But nothing felt like enough.

Because his success wasn't about *impact.*
It was about *proving someone wrong.*

And even when he hit $100K, the win didn't land.
He was still chasing an argument from four years ago.

That's the trick of revenge—it pushes you forward,
but never lets you feel arrived.

THE THREE EMOTIONS THAT FAKE LIKE PURPOSE

1. REGRET

"If I just hadn't done that…"
"I can't forgive myself."
"Maybe this will fix what I messed up."

Regret makes you *perform for redemption.*
You overwork. Overgive. Overcompensate.
Trying to cancel a past version of you that no longer exists.

But regret doesn't pay your future's rent.

It just keeps you living in a loop where nothing is ever enough.

2. GUILT

"I owe them this."
"They were there for me once."
"What kind of person would I be if I said no?"

Guilt makes you choose obligation over elevation.
You say "yes" when you want to say "nah."
You shrink so others don't feel small around you.
You stay where your soul no longer fits.

CONTROL THE PULSE

But guilt doesn't mean you're doing the right thing.
It just means your past still has a voice in your present.

3. REVENGE

"They're gonna see me shine."
"I'll post this just to let them know."
"I don't even want them—I just want them to miss me."

Revenge dresses itself in ambition.
But at the root? It's still painful.
You're still letting your enemy define your goalpost.

Which means—no matter how far you go,
they still own part of your story.

STORY 2: THE DAUGHTER WHO COULDN'T SAY NO

Lena took care of everybody.
She paid her mama's bills.
She let her little brother live with her for free.
She worked 50-hour weeks and still sent $200 back home every Friday.

Why?

Because she felt *guilty* for going to college while her siblings struggled.

She couldn't enjoy her wins.
She couldn't say no.
She didn't feel worthy of rest.

She told her therapist,
"Every time I eat good or buy something nice, I feel like I'm betraying where I came from."

That's how guilt hides.
Not in weakness.
But in overgiving.

CONTROL THE PULSE

YOU THINK YOU'RE MAKING PROGRESS... BUT WHO ARE YOU REALLY ANSWERING TO?

When your goals are built on:
- **Regret**, you move to erase.
- **Guilt**, you move to repay.
- **Revenge**, you move to prove.

But when your moves are built on **clarity**—you move to create.

That's the shift.

You're not here to undo the past.
You're here to build the future.
And no emotion—*no matter how deep*—should be driving the ship if it can't see the full map.

HOW TO SPOT WHEN THESE EMOTIONS ARE CONTROLLING YOU

Ask:

"If I remove the pain—do I still want this?"

Would I still build this business?
Would I still post that message?
Would I still say yes to this event?

"Am I doing this from alignment—or emotional debt?"

If you owe yourself success, cool.
But if you owe *someone else* your hustle?
You're still in chains.

"What happens if they never see it?"

Will I still be proud?
Or was this whole thing a silent scream for attention?

CONTROL THE PULSE

STORY 3: THE MAN WHO FORGAVE HIMSELF AND FINALLY RESTED

Omari had three kids and worked like he had six.
 Double shifts. Uber at night. Side hustles on weekends.

When asked why, he said,
 "I wasted too many years in the streets. I don't get to rest."

But one day his son looked at him and said,
 "Daddy, do you ever get tired of not being home?"

That cracked something.

He realized he wasn't just working hard—
 He was *punishing himself.*

Trying to earn forgiveness through exhaustion.

Now?
 He still works. But from **purpose**, not **penance.**
 He goes to games. Take rest days. Breathes without guilt.

Because *you can't parent or prosper from punishment.*

RELEASE THE DEBT—AND OWN THE FUTURE

You don't owe your pain anything.
 You don't owe the past another minute of your now.
 You don't have to post your healing for people who broke you.
 You don't have to grind so your old doubters see you on Forbes.

They were a chapter.
 You are the author.

Let your next move come from peace—not pain.
 From vision—not vengeance.

Narrator's Reflection:

CONTROL THE PULSE

You've done enough apologizing.
You've suffered enough silently.
You've posted enough "look at me now" quotes.

Now it's time to build for *you*—not to prove, repay, or punish.

Because regret, guilt, and revenge will always offer you *movement*—
But never *fulfillment.*

So pause.
Check your motive.
Then choose from power, not pain.

CHAPTER 10

WHO PROFITS FROM YOUR EMOTIONAL REACTIONS?

"Every Time You React Without Thinking, Somebody's Already Thought About How To Profit From It." — *Tierre Ford*

You're not weak.
You're targeted.

Your emotions?
They're not just *felt*—they're *mined.*

We live in a world that *studies*, *tracks*, *predicts*, and *profits* off your emotional spikes.

From the time you wake up to the time you scroll yourself to sleep, every reaction you have is being converted into someone else's paycheck.

You think it's just you feeling anxious, insecure, angry, or triggered?

**Nah.
That's business.**

STORY 1: THE SHOE DROP THAT WAS NEVER ABOUT SHOES

Jayden didn't plan to spend $300.
 But when he saw the limited-edition kicks dropping "for 24 hours only," his hands started sweating. His heart raced.

He clicked buy. Felt powerful—for about 15 minutes.

CONTROL THE PULSE

Then came the overdraft fee.
Then the stress.
Then the quiet shame.

That wasn't a shopping decision.
That was a **psychological play.**

The company created urgency.
Triggered FOMO.
Tapped into identity, ego, insecurity.

And cashed out.
Because Jayden wasn't a customer.
He was a *targeted emotional reaction.*

THE TRUTH: EMOTION IS MONETIZED

Let's break it down:

- **Fear sells security.**

Home systems. Insurance. Worry-based advertising.

- **Insecurity sells enhancement.**

Makeup. Weight loss. Plastic surgery. Designer brands.

- **Anger sells attention.**

Viral videos. Clickbait headlines. Divisive content.

- **Sadness sells comfort.**

Junk food. Streaming subscriptions. Temporary pleasures.

- **Ego sells identity.**

Car ads. Clothing lines. Luxury. Exclusivity.

You are being sold *solutions to emotions* all day long.
And if you're not aware, you'll keep buying temporary fixes to permanent problems.

CONTROL THE PULSE

THE DIGITAL MACHINE IS BUILT ON YOUR FEELS

Every scroll? Logged.
 Every pause? Analyzed.
 Every "like"? Profiled.

You don't get free content.
 You *are* the content.

If a post makes you mad, you stay longer.
 If it makes you sad, you scroll slower.
 If it makes you feel *not enough*, they know how to sell you "enough."

It's not a glitch.
 It's the **system**.

And if your emotions stay unguarded,
 you're not living life—you're being led through it.

STORY 2: THE ARGUMENT THAT BOOSTED THEIR ALGORITHM

Two influencers staged a breakup online.

Tears. Screenshots. Accusations.
 They both "went live."
 Their followers picked sides.

Overnight, both gained 200K followers.
 One launched a relationship podcast.
 The other dropped a self-love course.

It was fake.
 But the drama felt real.
 And feelings make you click.
 And clicks make them money.

Because **your emotional reaction is their strategy.**

CONTROL THE PULSE

EVEN PEOPLE PROFIT OFF YOUR EMOTIONS

It's not just corporations.
Sometimes the people around you win when you lose your center.

- Your ex texts just to see if they still have access.
- Your family guilt-trips you into staying small.
- Your boss manipulates your loyalty to work unpaid hours.
- That "friend" gives backhanded compliments to control your confidence.

Every time you react without awareness, someone gets what they wanted—and you get played.

WHO GAINS WHEN YOU LOSE CONTROL?

- Who benefits when you stay angry?
- Who profits when you stay broke from emotional spending?
- Who gets attention when you stay triggered and reactive online?
- Who feels powerful when you shrink yourself out of guilt?

Ask the question.
Follow the motive.
Because if there's a reaction,
there's always a return—for someone.

HOW TO BECOME EMOTIONALLY UN-PROFITABLE

1. Become boring to manipulation.
If drama doesn't move you, it loses its value.
If urgency doesn't scare you, sales drop.
If shade doesn't trigger you, the people throwing it look silly.

2. Ask: "Who is this reaction serving?"
Before you post, click, spend, or respond—pause.

CONTROL THE PULSE

Am I reacting from *me*—or from being played?

3. Take back your timeline.
Curate what you see.
Unfollow accounts that trigger unnecessary emotion.
Mute toxicity.
Protect your *mental economy.*

4. Practice emotional fasting.
One day a week: no purchases, no scrolling, no reacting.
Learn how much power you have when nobody is pulling your strings.

STORY 3: THE MAN WHO STOPPED TAKING THE BAIT

Quinton used to fall for every headline.
He'd rage-share. Argue in the comments.
Buy gear from causes he didn't understand.
He called it "being informed."
But it was emotional exhaustion disguised as activism.

One day, his daughter said,
"Daddy, why are you always mad at your phone?"

That did it.

He took 30 days offline.
Read books. Walked. Ate real food. Slept better.
And realized—*he'd been emotionally outsourced.*

Now? He still engages—but from *intention,* not *impulse.*

Because awareness is what turns victims of manipulation into masters of movement.

Narrator's Reflection:

There's power in pause.
There's profit in silence.
There's wealth in stillness.

CONTROL THE PULSE

When you stop reacting, you start ruling.

Because this world isn't just selling products.
It's selling *permission to own your mind.*

And when you reclaim that?
You don't just break free.
You become unshakable.

So next time something tries to pull you out of character, ask yourself one thing:

"Is this my emotion—or their business plan?"

CHAPTER 11

EMOTIONAL INTELLIGENCE VS. EMOTIONAL CONTROL

"Knowing how you feel is awareness. Choosing what to do with it is power." — *Tierre Ford*

Let's clear this up once and for all.

Just because you can name your emotions
doesn't mean you know what to *do* with them.

Just because you can talk about your pain
doesn't mean you've *mastered* it.

Welcome to the line between emotional intelligence…
and emotional control.

Because knowing you're angry is one thing.
Not slapping the table, not sending the text, not throwing the jab—that's something *else*.

Emotional intelligence is understanding your feelings.
Emotional control is leading them.

STORY 1: THE MAN WHO COULDN'T SHUT UP TO SAVE HIS JOB

Leon was brilliant.
He knew how to read a room. Could feel an energy shift in seconds.
But when he got criticized at work? He couldn't help himself.

He popped off.
Said what "needed to be said."
Stormed out of meetings.

CONTROL THE PULSE

Then came the pink slip.

His friend said,

"You're smart, bro. But smart ain't the same as strategic."

Leon had emotional intelligence.
But no emotional control.
So his talent couldn't protect him from his temper.

WHAT IS EMOTIONAL INTELLIGENCE?

It's the ability to:

- Recognize your emotions
- Understand why you feel them
- Identify emotional patterns in yourself and others
- Use that awareness to manage relationships

It's empathy. Self-awareness. Mental clarity.

But here's the problem:
Awareness without discipline still leads to destruction.

Knowing *why* you sabotage doesn't stop the sabotage—*unless you lead your emotions.*

That's emotional control.

WHAT IS EMOTIONAL CONTROL?

Emotional control is:

- Pausing when triggered
- Speaking when it's wise—not just when it's real
- Not letting temporary feelings create permanent consequences
- Holding yourself accountable for what you *choose* to act on

CONTROL THE PULSE

Control isn't suppression.
It's *selection*.

It's not "faking it."
It's being *faithful* to who you want to become—even when your emotions beg you to act wild.

STORY 2: THE TEXT SHE DIDN'T SEND

Renee found out he cheated.

She had receipts. Rage. A whole paragraph was drafted.

But something told her:

"You already have the truth. Why do you need the war?"

She deleted the message.
Blocked him. Went to Pilates.

She cried—but kept her crown.
Because emotional control is what lets her protect her future peace instead of fighting over past lies.

That wasn't weakness.
That was *maturity*.

THE DANGER OF ONLY HAVING ONE

If you only have emotional intelligence, you'll sound self-aware while still wrecking your life.
If you only have emotional control, you'll suppress your truth until it becomes an illness.

You need both.

- Feel it.
- Name it.
- Challenge it.

CONTROL THE PULSE

- Lead it.

That's the formula.

ARE YOU SMART WITH EMOTIONS OR JUST SPONTANEOUS WITH THEM?

Ask yourself:
- Do I know my triggers?
- Can I sit in discomfort without reacting?
- Do I give myself time to cool before I respond?
- Do I notice when my emotions are steering the car?

You don't need to "fix" emotions.
You need to *guide* them.

They're signals. Not instructions.
You're the one driving.

STORY 3: THE FATHER WHO BROKE THE CYCLE

Eric grew up getting yelled at for everything.

So when he had a son, he swore: "I'll never be that dad."

But one day, his kid dropped a full plate of food.
Eric stood up so fast the chair fell over.
His son flinched.

That moment broke him.
Not because he was angry—but because he *recognized* the fear on his son's face. A fear he once knew.

He stepped away. Cried. Then apologized.

He didn't just have awareness—he *used it to stop the cycle.*

That's emotional control.
That's how healing becomes legacy.

CONTROL THE PULSE

HOW TO BUILD EMOTIONAL CONTROL ON TOP OF INTELLIGENCE

1. Check your inner dialogue.
 What are you telling yourself when you feel disrespected, dismissed, unseen?

2. Choose time over tension.
 Give yourself a delay buffer. 10 minutes. One walk. One prayer. Then speak.

3. Practice neutral thinking.

"What's the most *useful* thought right now?"
 Not just the realest, but the one that serves peace.

4. Rehearse the outcome you want.
 What result are you aiming for?
 If your emotion can't help build it, don't let it lead.

Narrator's Reflection:

You don't have to react to every feeling.
 You don't have to perform your pain.
 You don't owe anybody your rage on display.

What you *do* owe is this:

To recognize your emotions without becoming their servant.
 To feel deeply, but respond wisely.
 To let your feelings rise—but your wisdom reigns.

That's when life shifts.

That's when emotional intelligence turns into emotional *mastery*.

CHAPTER 12

REFRAMING — CHANGE THE MEANING, CHANGE THE OUTCOME

"What Happened Is What Happened. What It *Meant* Is Up To You. And That's Where Your Freedom Lives." — *Tierre Ford*

Same situation.
Two different people.
Two different outcomes.

One gets broken.
The other gets built.

Why?

Not because life was fairer to one.
Not because pain picked favorites.
But because one of them knew how to reframe.

Reframing is the power to change the meaning you attach to a moment—so you change what that moment does to you.

Pain doesn't break you.
 The meaning you give it does.

STORY 1: THE GIRL WHO DIDN'T GET PICKED

Lani auditioned for the dance team.
 She practiced for weeks. Posted about it. Manifested it. Prayed.

She didn't make it.

Her old self would've collapsed—spiraled into "I'm not good enough."

CONTROL THE PULSE

But this time, she paused. She reframed.

"Maybe this isn't a rejection. Maybe it's a redirect."

So she applied to be the team's videographer. Got the role. Built her skills.
By the next year, she was running the brand. Now? She owns a digital agency.

The door that closed?
She didn't break down.
She built *around* it.

That's reframing.

WHAT IS REFRAMING?

Reframing is not lying to yourself.
It's **leading yourself.**

It's taking the same facts… and changing the story.

Not to escape.
But to *elevate*.

It's asking:

"How else can I see this?"
"What else could this mean?"
"How could this be working *for* me?"

When you reframe, you reclaim your power from pain.

WHY MEANING MATTERS MORE THAN MEMORY

Two people can go through the same breakup.

One says:

"They wasted my time."
They spiral into distrust and bitterness.

The other says:

CONTROL THE PULSE

"They taught me what I don't want."
They get clearer. Stronger. Wiser.

Same story.
Different frame.
One is stuck.
The other is free.

STORY 2: THE FELONY THAT BECAME A FOUNDATION

Andre went to prison at 22.
He lost four years to a system that didn't care.

But when he came out, he said:

"They took time, but they didn't take my voice."

He became a speaker.
Started mentoring at-risk youth.
Opened a nonprofit for returning citizens.

He reframed his sentence—not as punishment, but preparation.

Now when people ask about his past, he says:

"I was educated by the system… so I could teach them how to never return."

THE MOST POWERFUL REFRAMES IN LIFE

- **Rejection → Redirection**

You didn't lose. You got spared.

- **Failure → Feedback**

It didn't destroy you. It taught you.

- **Delay → Development**

You're not behind. You're being built.

- **Betrayal → Boundaries**

CONTROL THE PULSE

They didn't break you. They revealed themselves.

- **Loss → Launchpad**

What left you... leveled you up.

Every pain has potential—if you reframe it.

STORY 3: THE KID WHO GOT CUT FROM THE TEAM

Terrance didn't make the basketball squad.
Cried. Shut down. Didn't go to school for three days.

His uncle asked him,

"Do you want the game—or the applause?"

That question shifted everything.

He started practicing harder. No crowd. No claps. Just focus.

Next year, he made varsity.
Senior year? Captain.
College? Full scholarship.

He now tells every kid:

"That cut? It carved the version of me I needed."

Because not getting picked taught him how to *pick himself.*

HOW TO REFRAME IN THE MOMENT

1. Pause the panic.
Before spiraling, stop. Stillness invites perspective.

2. Ask new questions.
Instead of "Why me?" ask:

"What's this here to teach me?"
"How can this shape me—not just shake me?"

CONTROL THE PULSE

3. Flip the lens.
Imagine telling this story one year from now.
What's the empowering version?

4. Find the gift in the grit.
Even if it's not obvious now—search for growth, strength, or clarity.

REMEMBER THIS: PAIN IS A MESSAGE—NOT A DEFINITION

What hurt you wasn't designed to hold you.
You decide what stays a scar…
and what becomes a source of strength.

Because life will hand you the canvas.
But you pick the frame.

Narrator's Reflection:

You are not what happened to you.
You are what you *decide it meant.*

Reframing doesn't erase the truth.
It expands it.

So the next time life throws something heavy,
don't just catch it—*cut it into something sharper.*

Ask:

"How can I make this my teacher?"
"How can I turn this story into strategy?"

That's not delusion.
That's emotional brilliance.

CHAPTER 13

THE POWER OF PAUSE — MASTERING STILLNESS BEFORE ACTION

"Stillness Is Not The Absence Of Motion. It's The Presence Of Mastery." — *Tierre Ford*

In a world that claps for speed,
nobody teaches you how to *wait for wisdom.*

They praise the hustle.
They reward the reaction.
They glorify the grind.

But the most powerful move you can make?
Might be the one you don't make—*yet.*

That's the pause.
That's the stillness that separates survivors from strategists.

STORY 1: THE DEAL THAT ALMOST DESTROYED HIS BUSINESS

Devon was a self-made entrepreneur.
Smart. Driven. Hungry.

A major retailer offered him shelf space—but the deal was off balance.
Too fast. Too demanding. Too one-sided.

His team said take it. His ego said take it.
But his instinct whispered: *"Pause."*

He sat on it for 48 hours. Prayed. Slept. Listened.

Then he rewrote the proposal—and sent back a counter.

CONTROL THE PULSE

They accepted.
 Same shelf space. Better terms. Real power.

Because sometimes you don't win by moving first.
 You win by *waiting with vision.*

THE LIE: "IF YOU DON'T MOVE FAST, YOU'LL MISS IT."

That's how fear talks.

It tells you:

- "Say something now!"
- "Don't let them disrespect you!"
- "Buy it before it's gone!"
- "Respond or you'll look weak!"
- "Act before they act on you!"

But the truth is:
Anything that falls apart because you paused wasn't built right anyway.

Urgency is the mask of manipulation.
 Stillness is the soil of strength.

THE PAUSE IS NOT PASSIVITY—IT'S *PREPARATION*

Here's what the pause gives you:

- Clarity
- Control
- Composure
- Chess-player energy
- The space to think without pressure pulling your strings

Every time you pause before reacting, you **disarm the trap.**

CONTROL THE PULSE

STORY 2: THE TEXT SHE NEVER SENT

Marissa found out her friend was talking behind her back.
Her phone got hot in her hand.
She started typing a paragraph that would've gone *viral*.

But something told her:

"You don't need to defend your name. Let your character speak."

She turned her phone off.
Went to dinner with people who loved her.
Smiled like peace lived on her skin.

Two weeks later, the truth came out—without her ever responding.

That was the pause.
It didn't just protect her brand.
It *preserved her energy*.

WHAT HAPPENS WHEN YOU MASTER STILLNESS

- You stop leaking energy on nonsense
- You outgrow arguments you used to start
- You spot manipulation in real time
- You save your responses for things that *actually* matter
- You become unpredictable—in the best way

People won't know what moves you'll make next
because *you don't even move until you're ready*.

That's *power*.

WHEN TO PAUSE (EVEN WHEN YOU DON'T FEEL LIKE IT)

Pause when:

- You feel disrespected
- You want to post out of pain

CONTROL THE PULSE

- You're about to over-explain yourself
- You're tempted to buy for validation
- You're about to re-engage what you already healed from
- You're being rushed into a decision that doesn't sit right

The stronger the emotion—the longer the pause should be.

TOOLS FOR MASTERING THE PAUSE

1. Ask: "Is this emotion trying to protect me or expose me?"
Pause and sort the energy.

2. Use "The Window Rule"
Give every major decision a 24–72 hour window. If it's still right after stillness—it's real.

3. Create a "Pause Response"
Something you say when you feel the heat rise:

"I'm gonna sit with this first."
"Let me take a beat."
"I'll respond when I'm ready, not reactive."

4. Journal what the pause revealed.
Stillness doesn't just delay action.
It *downloads clarity.*

STORY 3: THE MAN WHO BUILT SILENCE INTO HIS MORNINGS

Reggie used to wake up in chaos.
Phone. News. Texts. Stress.

Until one day, he said:

"What if I gave myself 30 minutes of silence before I gave the world my energy?"

CONTROL THE PULSE

He started with five minutes.
 Then 10. Then 30.

Now?
 He doesn't speak to anyone before he's spoken to himself.

And his whole life moves slower—but hits harder.

Because when you *center before you serve,*
 you don't just survive the day—you *steer* it.

Narrator's Reflection:

Stillness isn't just for monks.
 It's for bosses.
 It's for mothers.
 It's for builders, leaders, lovers, healers, and hustlers.

It's for *you.*

Because when you pause,
 you don't just delay your reaction.
 You sharpen your response.
 You invite wisdom.
 You move like someone who's already arrived—even when you're still on the way.

Next time you feel the fire rise,
 before you react, before you reply, before you jump…

Pause.

Let the emotion pass through the gate of intention.

Then move like the master you're becoming.

CHAPTER 14

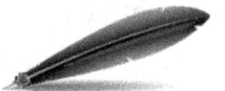

REFRAMING — CHANGE THE MEANING, CHANGE THE OUTCOME

"Life happens. But meaning? That's on you. Reframe the story—and you rewrite your ending." — *Tierre Ford*

The most dangerous thing you ever believed…
was the first story you told yourself about what hurt you.

- "They left, so I must not be enough."
- "I failed, so maybe I'm not meant to win."
- "They didn't choose me, so I must not be valuable."

That story—if you don't challenge it—becomes your blueprint.
And you build a life around someone else's damage.

That's why **reframing** is the key to freedom.
Because what happened can't change.
But what do you *make of it?*
That changes everything.

STORY 1: THE DROPOUT WHO TURNED DETENTION INTO DIRECTION

Jerome got kicked out his senior year.

He was labeled a "problem child."
Everyone said he'd end up locked up or laid out.

For a while, he believed it.
Until one day he asked himself:

CONTROL THE PULSE

"What if I wasn't failing school—what if school was failing me?"

He reframed his identity.
 Started reading books *he* picked. Studied financial literacy. Learned trades.
 Now he teaches kids the system was never built to serve.

Same story—new meaning.
 He's not a failure. He's a **blueprint rewriter.**

WHAT IS REFRAMING, REALLY?

It's the mental switch that turns:

- **Rejection** into *redirection*
- **Loss** into *launchpads*
- **Delays** into *development*
- **Trauma** into *testimony*
- **Mistakes** into *material*

Reframing isn't denial.
 It's a decision.

It's saying:

"I can't control what happened. But I *can* control what I do with it."

WHY MOST PEOPLE STAY STUCK IN THE WRONG FRAME

Because pain speaks first.
 And the pain is loud.

It tells you:

- "You'll always be like this."
- "Nobody cares."
- "You blew it."

CONTROL THE PULSE

- "They got over you."
- "You should've done better."

And instead of checking it, we *repeat it*.
Until it becomes an identity.

But what if pain lied?
What if there was another version of the story that still honors the truth—without chaining you to it?

STORY 2: THE DIVORCEE WHO FOUND HERSELF IN THE MIRROR

Maya got divorced after 14 years.

At first, all she saw was failure.
The years "wasted." The family is "broken." The fear of starting over.

Then her therapist asked:

"What if you didn't fail your marriage?
What if you graduated from it?"

That line cracked something wide open.

She reframed her experience.
Started speaking to women about releasing shame.
Taught her daughters that leaving *with dignity* is just as powerful as staying *out of fear*.

She didn't hide her story.
She *reframed it into healing*.

THE REFRAME ISN'T FOR THE PAST. IT'S FOR YOUR FUTURE.

Because the story you repeat…
Becomes the path you walk.

CONTROL THE PULSE

And the path you walk...
Decide who you become.

So if the story sounds like suffering on repeat,
you've got to flip the narrative.

HOW TO REFRAME IN REAL TIME

1. Ask, "What else could this mean?"
Shift from victimhood to possibility.

2. Zoom out.
Will this matter in 6 months? 6 years?
What's the 30,000-foot view?

3. Say it out loud.
"This happened. But I'm not done."
"This hurt—but it's not my home."
"This loss is teaching me something I didn't want—but may need."

4. Speak from the future.
What will the wiser version of you say about this season?

Write from there.

STORY 3: THE BOY WHO WAS BULLIED INTO PURPOSE

Darius was overweight, quiet, and called every name in the book.

He hated school. Hated mirrors. Hated himself.
Until he reframed the hate.

He started lifting weights—not for looks, but for *discipline*.
Started running—not to escape—but to *arrive*.
Eventually became a trainer and mentor to kids who felt invisible.

He says now:

"The same pain that almost killed me... became the voice I use to save others."

CONTROL THE PULSE

That's the power of reframing.
 You turn wounds into weapons.
 Scars into stories.
 And weakness into your *why*.

Narrator's Reflection:

You don't need to fake it.
 You don't need to forget it.
 But you *do* need to **frame it right.**

Because your past can either anchor you—or launch you.

And that power? It's in the lens.
 Not the event.
 Not the pain.
 Not the person.

You.

Next time life hits you hard,
 don't just ask, "Why me?"

Ask:

"How can I reframe this to reveal the version of me that's rising?"

That's how you stop reliving pain
 and start *rebuilding from it.*

CONTROL THE PULSE

CHAPTER 15

BECOMING THE CEO OF YOUR LIFE

"Your life is an organization. You're either running it like a boss—or letting your emotions run it into the ground."
— *Tierre Ford*

You don't need more motivation.
You need *management.*

Because feelings are loud.
Temptation is sneaky.
And life? Life is a full-time business.

That's why you need to shift—from *reacting like an employee* to *executing like a CEO.*

You are the chief executive officer of **your mind**, **your money**, **your habits**, and **your peace**.

Start acting like it.

STORY 1: THE WOMAN WHO TOOK HER LIFE OFF AUTO-PILOT

Keisha used to wake up late, scroll her phone, rush to work, eat random food, ignore her bank account, then wonder why her life felt chaotic.

One night she wrote this in her journal:

"If my life was a company, I'd fire me."

That hit was different.

CONTROL THE PULSE

So she flipped it.

She created a morning meeting with herself.
 Set daily agendas. Made vision her mission statement.
 Cut toxic people like poor-performing vendors.
 Started asking:

"Does this serve the company of *me*?"

Six months later—new job, better energy, savings growing, boundaries locked.

She didn't just glow up.
 She *took the seat at the head of her own table.*

WHAT IT MEANS TO BE THE CEO OF YOUR LIFE

- You stop waiting for permission
- You audit your emotions like budgets
- You fire thoughts that don't bring returns
- You set policy based on peace, not pressure
- You don't explain executive decisions to emotional interns

Being CEO isn't about control.
 It's about *clarity.*

You decide what's worth your time, what's draining your energy, and what no longer belongs on your calendar—or in your heart.

YOUR EMOTIONS ARE DEPARTMENTS—BUT NOT THE CEO

Anger? Department.
Fear? Department.
Desire? Department.
Pride? Department.

But none of them run the company.

CONTROL THE PULSE

You do.

And if you let one department take over the whole operation, you'll crash.

The CEO listens—but doesn't obey without strategy.

STORY 2: THE MAN WHO STOPPED BEING THE INTERN IN HIS OWN LIFE

Tariq said yes to everything.

Last-minute favors. People's problems. Parties he didn't want to go to.
 He called it "being supportive."

But his goals were starving.

One night he looked at his calendar and realized—none of it was about *him*.

He said:

"I'm working in everyone else's office, and my own desk is empty."

So he started managing his energy like a resource.

"No is a policy now."
"Silence is a leadership tool."
"I'm not ignoring people—I'm prioritizing my mission."

That's what happens when the intern clocks out... and the *executive shows up*.

SIGNS YOU'RE NOT ACTING LIKE YOUR OWN CEO

- You wake up reacting, not directing
- You say yes to things that drain you
- You let guilt run your schedule

CONTROL THE PULSE

- You're too tired to work on your goals—but always available for distractions
- You spend like a customer, not like an owner

That's not leadership.
That's emotional outsourcing.

THE CEO CHECKLIST: HOW TO RUN YOU INC.

1. Create a Vision Statement

"What does success look like *for me* in this season?"
Clarity creates consistency.

2. Run Daily Meetings

Morning check-in. Intentional start. Mental agenda.

"What are we focused on today? What energy is required? What do we cut?"

3. Set Performance Metrics

Track your habits. Not just your hustle.
What's growing? What's draining? What's delaying the mission?

4. Audit People and Patterns Quarterly

If they don't align with your vision, they don't get stock options.

5. Pay Yourself First

Your time. Your peace. Your growth. Non-negotiable.
Before the world collects—you invest in you.

STORY 3: THE TEEN WHO STARTED THINKING LIKE A TYCOON

Jahlil was 17 with dreams but no direction.

Until his mentor asked:

"If your life was a brand, what would it stand for?
And would you hire the version of you living today to run it?"

CONTROL THE PULSE

That changed everything.

He made a binder—labeled it "CEO of Me."
Tracked goals. Income. Mindset shifts. People he had to outgrow. Every week, he reviewed his life like a business plan.

Now? He runs a YouTube channel teaching other teens how to build their inner boardroom before they build their brand.

That's legacy thinking.
That's *executive energy*.

Narrator's Reflection:

You are not just a person.
You are a walking organization.
You are structured. Vision. Discipline. Value.

But only if you *run it that way*.

So next time life gets noisy…
when emotions pull, when guilt knocks, when distractions offer "quick wins"…

Ask yourself:

"Is this decision in alignment with the company I'm building?"

If not, the answer is simple:
Respectfully, no.
The CEO has spoken.

CHAPTER 16

REPLACING EMOTION WITH FRAMEWORKS

"Feelings fade. Frameworks last. When life gets loud, structure speaks louder than stress." — *Tierre Ford*

Here's the hard truth:
Most people don't lack motivation.
They lack *systems*.

They say:

- "I just didn't feel like it."
- "Something came up."
- "I was off today."

But feelings aren't a strategy.
You can't build anything strong on a foundation of mood swings.

That's why frameworks matter.

Because frameworks are *anchors*.
They don't care if you're tired, triggered, or tempted.

They don't ask how you feel.
They ask: *What's the plan?*

STORY 1: THE WRITER WHO COULDN'T FINISH A BOOK

Tanya wanted to write a novel.
Every few weeks she got inspired—wrote for hours—then stopped.

Her emotion kept saying:

CONTROL THE PULSE

"You'll get back to it when it feels right."

Two years passed.
Still no book.

Then she learned about writing frameworks:
Daily word count. Non-negotiable writing blocks. Deadline sprints. Not glamorous. Not emotional. Just structure.

Six months later—book done.
Not because inspiration struck—but because *the system didn't care if it did or didn't.*

WHAT IS FRAMEWORK?

A framework is a repeatable structure that guides decision-making *without needing emotion to show up.*

It's the difference between:

- Winging it… vs. Winning with consistency
- Emotional reasoning… vs. Strategic execution
- Hoping to do better… vs. Designing your days for better

Frameworks don't kill creativity.
They protect it from chaos.

EMOTION AS A DECISION TOOL: WHY IT FAILS

- It's inconsistent
- It's impulsive
- It's reactive, not reflective
- It makes excuses sound like logic
- It turns setbacks into shutdowns

Without a framework, you're at the mercy of:

- Your hormones

CONTROL THE PULSE

- Your environment
- Your past
- Your triggers
- Other people's moods

You're not *leading* your life.
You're *negotiating* with it.

STORY 2: THE MAN WHO STOPPED TRUSTING MOTIVATION

Reggie was trying to lose 30 pounds.

He bought supplements. Watched fitness influencers. Tried five different programs.
But his results came and went—with his mood.

Then he met a coach who said:

"We don't chase motivation here. We follow frameworks."

Meal prep system. Workout schedule. Non-negotiable sleep rules. Hydration plan.
Simple. Tight. Boring to some.
But for Reggie? *It worked.*

Because now, *motivation wasn't required.*
Execution was automatic.

That's how emotion got replaced—with *engineering*.

FRAMEWORKS TO REPLACE EMOTIONAL DECISION-MAKING

1. The "10–10–10" Rule

Before making a decision, ask:

CONTROL THE PULSE

How will I feel about this in 10 minutes?
 10 days?
 10 months?

It forces emotional distance and future thinking.

2. The "Yes-If" Filter

Don't say yes unless it meets pre-set criteria:

Does it align with my values?
 Does it fit my calendar?
 Does it serve my future?

If not? *It's a no.*

3. Daily 3-Wins Framework

Start every day by identifying:

- 1 thing for the mind
- 1 thing for the mission
- 1 thing for momentum

This builds focus—no matter how you feel.

4. "Default Day" Scheduling

Design a go-to structure for days when energy is low.
 A fallback plan > emotional surrender.

STORY 3: THE SINGLE MOM WHO MADE STRUCTURE HER SUPERPOWER

Ayanna had two kids, two jobs, and a dream to build a side hustle.

Every time life hit hard, she used to say:

"I just can't do this right now."

But then she built a framework.

- Mondays = Outreach

CONTROL THE PULSE

- Tuesdays = Content
- Wednesdays = Admin
- Thursdays = Learning
- Fridays = Review

She didn't wait to *feel inspired*.
She just followed the system.

Now she's not guessing how to succeed—she's *executing success like a schedule*.

WHY FRAMEWORKS CREATE FREEDOM, NOT CAGES

People fear structure because they think it kills creativity.

But real talk?

Chaos is not creativity.
Chaos is exhaustion with prettier language.

Frameworks create mental bandwidth.
They reduce decision fatigue.
They make success a math problem—not a mystery.

Emotion burns fuel.
Frameworks build systems that *run even when you don't feel like running*.

Narrator's Reflection:

You're not failing because you're not smart.
You're not failing because you don't care.
You're failing because *emotion keeps interrupting execution*.

And until you build frameworks that work—
you'll keep chasing *feeling good* instead of building something great.

So ask yourself:

CONTROL THE PULSE

"What's the system behind the success I want?"
 "And where am I still hoping my emotions will carry me where only structure can?"

Because this next version of you?
 It doesn't need mood swings.
 It needs *models*.

CHAPTER 17

DETACH, DON'T DISCONNECT

"You don't have to stop caring. You just have to stop carrying everything." — *Tierre Ford*

There's a difference between *protecting your peace* and *building a wall that keeps everything out—including growth.*

Some people detach by becoming distant.
They disappear.
Stop talking.
Stop showing up.
Call it "peace," but it's really just an emotional *shutdown.*

That's disconnection.

True detachment isn't about quitting—it's about *releasing responsibility for things that were never yours to begin with.*

You don't disconnect from love.
You detach from *attachment to outcomes you can't control.*

STORY 1: THE WOMAN WHO LOVED HARD—AND LOST HERSELF

Tasha loved deeply.
Too deeply.
She bent for people. Broke for people. Stayed for people who wouldn't stay for her.

She thought,

CONTROL THE PULSE

"If I let go, I'm giving up."
"If I detach, I'm being cold."

But every time she overextended, she shrank.
Until she didn't recognize herself.

Her therapist told her:

"You're not abandoning them. You're choosing not to abandon yourself."

That line became her mirror.
She started responding with boundaries. Not silence.
She stayed soft—but stopped leaking her soul.

That's *detachment.*
Still loving. Still present. But **centered.**

WHAT DETACHMENT REALLY MEANS

- Detachment is staying grounded even when everything around you shakes.
- Detachment is loving people without managing their choices.
- Detachment is showing up with care—but not chasing closure.
- Detachment is releasing the outcome without surrendering your integrity.

It's not "cutting off."
It's *cutting loose*—from emotional contracts you didn't sign.

DISCONNECTION IS A DEFENSE MECHANISM.
DETACHMENT IS A DISCIPLINE.

When people get hurt, they tend to go to extremes:

- **Disconnect:**

CONTROL THE PULSE

"I'm done with everyone."
"I don't feel anything anymore."
"I don't need anybody."

- **Detach:**

"I still care, but I care *from alignment.*"
"I release what's not mine to fix."
"I love you—but I won't lose myself again."

Disconnection numbs.
Detachment *heals.*

STORY 2: THE MAN WHO WANTED TO FIX EVERYONE

Jeremiah had a savior complex.

He loaned money he didn't have.
Gave advice no one followed.
Stayed available 24/7.
Then got mad when no one showed up for *him.*

One day, he asked:

"Why do I always feel empty after I help people?"

The answer:
He wasn't helping—he was *overextending out of guilt.*

So he changed the approach:

- Started asking if people wanted help before offering it
- Waited until asked
- Gave from overflow, not from exhaustion

Now he says:

"I stopped bleeding for people who just needed a Band-Aid."

That's the *wisdom of detachment.*

CONTROL THE PULSE

HOW TO DETACH WITHOUT LOSING YOUR HUMANITY

1. Identify what's actually yours
If it's someone else's behavior, choices, feelings, or growth—it's *not* yours.

2. Pause before absorbing
When someone dumps emotion on you, ask:

"Is this for me to carry... or just to witness?"

3. Define your energy budget
Don't spend more emotional labor than you can afford.
Just because they're hurting doesn't mean you have to hemorrhage.

4. Speak from the center, not the edge
You don't have to ghost. You don't have to rage.
You can say:

"I care. But I won't compromise my peace to prove it."

STORY 3: THE FRIEND WHO LET GO WITHOUT MAKING A SCENE

Alisha and Monica had been close for years.
But lately, it felt one-sided.
No calls unless she called. No love unless she showed up first.

She didn't unfollow. Didn't post a thread. Didn't call her out.

She just... stepped back.
No anger. No cold shoulder. Just *alignment*.

When asked what happened, she said:

"Nothing bad. Just nothing balanced."

That's how detachment moves.
Quiet. Clean. Powerful.

DETACHMENT IS A SIGN OF GROWTH—NOT COLDNESS

CONTROL THE PULSE

You don't detach because you stopped loving.
 You detach because you finally started loving *yourself* with the same energy.

You don't detach because you stopped caring.
 You detach because you care enough to stop *losing your peace* every time someone else spins.

You don't detach because you gave up.
 You detach because you woke up.

Narrator's Reflection:

This is your permission:
 To let go without guilt.
 To say "not mine" without shame.
 To walk away *centered*, not cold.

Because being emotionally responsible doesn't mean being emotionally available to everyone at all times.

Next time someone tries to pull you into their storm—
 stand still in your peace and remember:

"I'm not cold.
 I'm just not carrying what isn't mine anymore."

CONTROL THE PULSE

CHAPTER 18

MENTAL MODELS OF BILLIONAIRES — THINKING BIGGER THAN EMOTION

"The difference between the average mind and the billionaire mind is this—one reacts to problems emotionally, the other solves them systematically." — *Tierre Ford*

Most people make decisions from emotion.
Billionaires make decisions from **models.**

They don't ask,

"How do I feel about this today?"

They ask,

"What system am I using to evaluate this—and what are the second-order consequences?"

Because emotion is a moment.
But systems are *scalable.*

And once you start thinking like that?
Everything changes.

STORY 1: THE DEAL THAT DIDN'T FEEL RIGHT—BUT WORKED ANYWAY

Andre had a chance to invest in a logistics company.
It didn't "excite" him.
Didn't look sexy. Didn't scream fast profit.

But the model was airtight.
Revenue predictable. Supply chain lean. Margins solid.

CONTROL THE PULSE

He didn't go with his *gut*. He went with the *framework*.

Five years later?
That boring investment made more money than all his "passion plays" combined.

That's billionaire thinking:

"Feelings are for the surface. Frameworks are for the foundation."

WHAT IS A MENTAL MODEL?

A mental model is a tool for understanding how the world works—*without* needing emotion to guide you.

It's a thinking lens. A shortcut to wisdom. A repeatable way of viewing decisions.

Billionaires don't guess.
They don't ride mood waves.
They use mental models to stay clear when life gets complex.

TOP MENTAL MODELS BILLIONAIRES USE (THAT YOU CAN TOO)

1. First Principles Thinking

Break everything down to what's *undeniably true*—then rebuild from there.

Elon Musk didn't say, "Cars are too expensive."
He said, "What are the base parts of a car? Can we source and build them cheaper?"

Use this when: You're stuck repeating what everyone else does.

2. Opportunity Cost

Every choice costs you *what you didn't choose*.
So the question is never "Is this good?"
It's "Is this better than everything else I could be doing with this time, money, or energy?"

CONTROL THE PULSE

Use this when: You're choosing between options that all *seem* good.

3. Inversion Thinking

Instead of asking, "How do I succeed?"
 Ask, "How do I *fail*—and how do I avoid those mistakes?"

Use this when: You want clarity fast.

"How do I destroy my finances? Spend emotionally, avoid saving, stay in debt."
 Now invert it.

4. Second-Order Thinking

Don't just think about the *immediate* result—think two or three steps ahead.

"If I do this… what will that lead to?"
 "And then what?"

Use this when: You're tempted to choose quick wins over long-term plays.

5. Circle of Competence

Only make moves inside your *knowledge zone.*
 If you don't know—don't guess. Learn or ask an expert.

Use this when: You're getting caught up in hype or trends.

STORY 2: THE WOMAN WHO STOPPED TRUSTING HER MOOD TO BUILD HER BRAND

Destiny used to run her business based on how she felt.

If she was up, she posted. If she was down, she ghosted.
 If she felt confident, she pitched. If not, she "took a mental break."

Her mentor said:

"Do you want this to be a business or a diary?"

CONTROL THE PULSE

That stung. But it landed.

She started using systems—content calendars, pitch frameworks, pricing ladders.

Now her emotions don't lead the business—her model does.

And the money? It's more *predictable* than her feelings ever were.

THE BIGGEST SHIFT: EMOTIONS ARE DATA, NOT DIRECTIONS

Billionaires don't ignore emotions.
They just **don't obey them.**

They use feelings as *indicators*, not instructions.

- "I feel nervous" → That means this matters.
- "I feel impatient" → That's a sign I need a timeline.
- "I feel excited" → Pause and verify before jumping.

They don't let the dopamine make the decision.
They run the data. Then decide.

HOW TO START THINKING LIKE A HIGH-LEVEL MIND TODAY

1. Replace Feelings with Filters
Ask:

"What system am I using to decide this?"

If you don't have one, you're relying on emotion.

2. Document Decisions
Track what worked and what didn't. Build a decision archive.
Success leaves *trails*—but only if you keep score.

3. Create a Mental Model Bank
Start collecting models that fit your life:
Time use, health decisions, money, love, boundaries.

CONTROL THE PULSE

Think of them like apps—*you choose which one to run.*

4. Use Logic Before Action
One-minute pause.
Run the emotion through a question filter.
Then choose.

STORY 3: THE MOTHER WHO STARTED THINKING LIKE A PORTFOLIO MANAGER

April was running herself into the ground.
Single mom. Trying to hustle. Always emotionally burnt out.

Then she read:

"Energy is an investment—manage it like a portfolio."

So she did.

- High-return people = priority
- Emotionally expensive situations = exit
- Sleep = non-negotiable
- Downtime = scheduled
- Crisis = handled with protocols, not panic

She said:

"I stopped managing chaos like a mom… and started managing my life like a CEO."

And everything changed.

Narrator's Reflection:

You don't have to be a billionaire to think like one.
 You just have to stop solving million-dollar problems with mood-based methods.

Feelings are valid.
But your *framework* decides your future.

CONTROL THE PULSE

So next time you're overwhelmed, uncertain, or stuck in your head, ask yourself:

"What model can I run—so I don't have to trust a feeling to lead me?"

Because emotions change.
 But systems?
 Systems *scale*.

CHAPTER 19

TRAINING YOUR BRAIN TO THINK IN OUTCOMES, NOT REACTIONS

"The most powerful people don't move fast. They move with purpose." — Tierre Ford

We all know what it feels like to react.

You see something.
Feel something.
Say something.
Do something.

And later... regret it.

Reaction is easy. It's automatic.
You touch a hot stove, you pull away. That's survival.

But you're not here to survive anymore.
You're here to **build**.
And builders don't just react—they **design**.

To get what you really want—health, wealth, peace, power—you have to train your brain to stop chasing the moment... and start serving the mission.

WHY OUTCOME THINKING IS A SUPERPOWER

Most people are emotionally hijacked by what's right in front of them. They make snap decisions based on fear, excitement, or pressure—and then spend weeks, months, or years cleaning up the mess.

CONTROL THE PULSE

Outcome thinkers do the opposite.

They ask, *"What's the end goal?"*
Then they make moves that serve that goal—even if it doesn't feel great right now.

This is what separates people who stay stuck from people who level up.

The stuck say, "What should I do right now?"
The builders say, "What decision moves me closer to where I said I want to be?"

REAL LIFE: THE POWER OF THE PAUSE

Tyrese used to be impulsive.

If someone disrespected him, he fired back.
If money got tight, he spent more trying to look rich.
If a woman didn't text back, he'd blow up her phone or ghost her completely.

He was always reacting—emotionally, immediately.

One day, an older mentor pulled him aside and said:

"You keep crashing into walls and wondering why life hurts. Slow down. Ask yourself what you actually want before you move."

Tyrese started pausing. Just ten seconds.
Before replying.
Before spending.
Before walking away.

It wasn't instant, but over time, he saw the power of waiting just long enough to ask:
"What result am I really after?"

Not revenge. Not attention. Not temporary relief.
He wanted peace. Stability. Legacy.
That meant changing how he *thought*—not just how he reacted.

CONTROL THE PULSE

TEACHING MOMENT: THE POWER OF OUTCOME THINKING

Start with this shift:
Don't just act. Aim.

Outcome-based thinking means every move is measured against the result you want. You're not responding to the moment—you're responding to the *mission*.

When you feel the urge to act emotionally, practice asking these instead:

- What do I want this to lead to?
- Will this bring me closer to or further from the life I'm building?
- Is this response for my growth, or just to soothe my ego?

STORY: FROM MESSY MOVES TO MASTER PLANS

Janelle ran her business like a mood ring.

If she felt good, she created.
If she felt ignored online, she shut down.
If sales were low, she panicked and dropped prices to feel productive.

She didn't realize she was running her business from an emotional place—not a strategic one.

A friend challenged her to treat her business like a project manager would.
Set clear outcomes.
Track progress weekly.
Create SOPs (Standard Operating Procedures) for content, outreach, and fulfillment.

At first, it felt stiff. Unnatural.
But soon she noticed:

CONTROL THE PULSE

Her income grew.
Her confidence grew.
And her emotions stopped swinging as wildly—because now, she had **structure.**

Outcome thinking brought her peace.
And peace became profitable.

MAKE IT PRACTICAL: SHIFTING FROM REACTION TO RESULT

Here's how to start training your brain, daily:

1. Name the Outcome Before You Move

Before you answer the call. Before you reply to the DM. Before you buy the thing.
Pause. Ask: *"What result do I want here?"*

Even thirty seconds of clarity can save you thirty days of damage.

2. Create Default Moves That Serve the Long-Term

If you're tired, your default might be to scroll or snack.
If you're triggered, your default might be to argue or shut down.

Change that.

Build new defaults:

- When stressed, I journal or walk.
- When confused, I seek counsel, not comfort.
- When tempted, I recheck the outcome.

3. Review Your Choices Every Night

Take five minutes.
Ask: Did my decisions today reflect the future I'm trying to build?

This reflection sharpens your aim for tomorrow.

CONTROL THE PULSE

STORY: THE SILENCE THAT BUILT STRENGTH

Devin got ghosted by someone he cared about.
 Every part of him wanted to lash out. Say something petty. Post something to get their attention.
 He opened Instagram. Then paused.

He asked himself,
 "What's my real goal here? Peace? Progress? Power? Or payback?"

He closed the app. Took a breath. Went for a run.

He realized that mastering outcomes didn't always mean doing something.
 Sometimes it meant doing *nothing*—on purpose.

That night, he felt stronger. Not because he won an argument—but because he *chose himself* over chaos.

That's emotional evolution.

REAL GROWTH = RESPONDING WITH VISION, NOT VOLUME

You don't get stronger by reacting faster.
 You get stronger by *slowing down* long enough to respond with vision.

Next time the moment gets loud, your emotions swell, and your ego wants to jump—remember:

You don't owe anyone your impulse.
 You owe yourself your outcome.

So train your brain like a sniper—clear target, steady hand.
 Because that's how goals get hit. That's how legacy is built.

Narrator's Reflection:

CONTROL THE PULSE

It's easy to stay stuck in reaction mode.
 But reaction mode will never build you a meaningful life—it only builds you a history of regret.

Train your brain to ask one simple thing:
 "Where is this decision taking me?"

If it's not forward, you already know the answer.

You're not here to be emotionally clever.
 You're here to be *strategically clear.*

CONTROL THE PULSE

CHAPTER 20

UNDERSTANDING DELAYED GRATIFICATION — PLAYING LONG TO WIN STRONG

"Every shortcut steals from the version of you that could've had it all." — *Tierre Ford*

Let's get one thing clear:
In a world trained to chase fast likes, fast checks, fast love—
slowness is rebellion.

But every real win you've ever wanted?
It lives behind the door marked *"Wait."*

Not because the world is against you.
But because anything worth keeping **demands development**.

Delayed gratification isn't punishment.
It's the strategy of visionaries.

FAST FEELS GOOD—BUT IT RARELY LASTS

Scrolling feels good.
Fast food feels good.
Impulse buys feel good.
Revenge feels good—for about ten seconds.

But the high always fades.
And when it does, you're left with the consequences.

That's the trap: the world rewards *speed* in the short-term, but only *strategy* wins long-term.

CONTROL THE PULSE

STORY: WHEN LISA WALKED AWAY FROM QUICK CASH

Lisa was offered a spot in a shady crypto pump-and-dump scheme.
Fast money. Easy return. Everyone around her said, "It's just business."

But something in her gut told her this wasn't the kind of win she wanted tied to her name.

So she passed.

Six months later, the feds raided the operation.
Indictments flew.
Reputations burned.

Lisa didn't just save money—she kept her peace.
Her *name* stayed clean.
And her long-term business? Still rising.

She said,

"I'd rather build slowly with roots than blow up fast and fall apart."

That's delayed gratification in motion: **choosing alignment over adrenaline.**

WHY MOST PEOPLE CAN'T WAIT (AND HOW TO TRAIN YOURSELF TO DO IT)

We've been wired to chase the *immediate reward*. It's survival biology.

But you're not surviving anymore—you're building a legacy.
Which means you have to rewire.

Here's how:

1. Make Waiting a Skill, Not a Struggle

Stop saying "be patient" like it's punishment.
Start seeing it as a weapon.

CONTROL THE PULSE

Waiting with intention is what separates the visionary from the impulsive.

2. Practice Saying No to the Good So You Can Say Yes to the Great

Sometimes what's offered isn't bad—it's just not *best*.

Mature people don't settle because it's available.
They hold out because they're *anchored* in the outcome.

3. Create Rituals That Reward the Process, Not Just the Result

Set up small wins that reflect big discipline.

Not just the deal closing—but the consistent outreach.
Not just the weight loss—but the gym streak.
Not just the launch—but the quiet nights building in the dark.

Celebrate endurance.

STORY: THE GUY WHO WOULDN'T FLEX TIL THE FOUNDATION WAS BUILT

Darius worked quietly.

No flash.
No show.
Just brick-by-brick consistency—investing, learning, saving, building.

People clowned him.

"Are you still driving that old car?"
"Still living in that basic apartment?"
"You ain't even poppin'."

But when the pandemic hit and half his circle fell off, Darius was untouched.
Paid off. Leveled up. Bought two rentals while the market dipped.

They didn't laugh after that.

CONTROL THE PULSE

He said,

"I wasn't chasing applause. I was building freedom."

Delayed gratification turned him into a fortress.

REAL TALK: IF YOU CAN'T WAIT, YOU CAN'T WIN

Every rich person waited:

- On compound interest
- On market cycles
- On brand reputation
- On self-discipline

Every strong relationship waited:

- On trust to deepen
- On egos to drop
- On the right timing
- On commitment to mature

Every healthy body waited:

- On habits to kick in
- On cravings to pass
- On daily reps that nobody saw

And every **whole** person waited:

- To heal
- To understand
- To grow
- To arrive

There is no version of the real you that gets there instantly.

CONTROL THE PULSE

HOW TO MAKE DELAYED GRATIFICATION WORK FOR YOU (NOT AGAINST YOU)

Create vision so clear it makes quitting embarrassing.
When your long-term goal is in focus, short-term temptations feel small.

Remind yourself: the joy of reaping always outweighs the thrill of rushing.
Because when it's *really* yours, you don't have to explain it. It shows.

Keep score with milestones, not dopamine.
Don't track how good you feel—track how far you've come.

STORY: THE WOMAN WHO TURNED DOWN A RING TO SAY YES TO HERSELF

Jasmine was offered a proposal.
Nice guy. Decent job. Comfortable life.
Everyone said she should go for it.

But deep down, she knew: it wasn't her dream—it was her fear of being alone.

So she walked.

She built her business. Found her rhythm. Traveling. Evolved.
Years later, she met someone who matched *everything* she grew into.

And this time, she said yes with no doubt.

She said,

"I didn't wait on him—I waited *for me* to become her."

And that made all the difference.

Narrator's Reflection:

CONTROL THE PULSE

Fast will always tempt you.
 But strong? Strong takes time.

This is your reminder:
 If you want fruit that lasts, you plant deeper roots.
 If you want results that change lives, you stretch the timeline.

You don't have to rush.
 You just have to keep moving—on purpose.

Let the world run on speed.
 You?
 You're running on strategy.

CONTROL THE PULSE

CHAPTER 21

EMOTIONAL SPENDING VS. STRATEGIC INVESTING

"If it cost you clarity, peace, or progress—it wasn't a purchase. It was a payment for avoiding what really needed to be faced." —
Tierre Ford

We've all been there.
Tired. Frustrated. Heart aching. Mind overloaded.

So we *buy something.*

New kicks. A trip. Jewelry. A fancy dinner.
Maybe something small—just enough to feel alive again.

But let's be honest...

You weren't shopping.
You were soothing.

You weren't investing.
You were reacting.

And if we don't check this emotional pattern, it becomes a trap disguised as "treating yourself."

THE HIGH-COST LOW-RETURN HABIT

Emotional spending is one of the easiest addictions to hide.
Because it's praised. It's normalized.
You get likes. Compliments. Even envy.

But what you don't see?

CONTROL THE PULSE

The growing credit card balances.
The emergency fund you never built.
The feeling of being in control slipping further away.

Because every time you trade discipline for dopamine, you shrink your financial future just to survive the day.

STORY: THE SHIRT THAT COST HIM A YEAR

Tyrell bought a $750 designer hoodie on a day he felt invisible.

He said it made him feel "seen," like he belonged.

For a few weeks, it worked.

Then his car broke down.
He didn't have savings.
He had to Uber to work for months.
That $750 could've fixed the car *and* started an emergency fund.

He told a friend,

"I spent to feel important. Now I feel stuck."

That's emotional spending: a temporary solution that creates permanent setbacks.

WHY STRATEGIC INVESTING FEELS HARD—AT FIRST

Strategic investing doesn't give you a rush.
It gives you a roadmap.

- Buying stocks? No instant thrill.
- Putting money into a course? No applause.
- Delaying a purchase to build credit? No flex.

But here's the secret:
Strategic investing feels boring now... but becomes freedom later.

CONTROL THE PULSE

Emotional spending feels powerful now... but becomes pressure later.

It's not about deprivation—it's about **direction.**

THE SHIFT: FROM IMPULSE TO INTENTION

Here's how you begin:

1. Feel the Feeling—But Don't Fund It

It's okay to feel empty, lonely, and overlooked.
But don't let your wallet try to fix your soul.

Feel it. Acknowledge it.
Then ask, *"What would serve me tomorrow, not just tonight?"*

2. Set a 24-Hour Rule for Purchases

If it's not food, gas, or bills—wait.
Give your brain time to shift from emotion to logic.

You'll be shocked how many "must-haves" become "I'm glad I didn't."

3. Tie Every Dollar to a Destination

Before you swipe, ask:
"Does this build me or bury me?"

- Does this move me toward ownership?
- Does this secure my future self?
- Will I be proud of this choice next year?

If the answer is no—it's a no.

STORY: THE WOMAN WHO INVESTED IN HER FUTURE SELF

Camille used to spend $400 a month on things that didn't last—fast fashion, drinks, constant upgrades.

CONTROL THE PULSE

Then she did something radical.

She tracked every dollar.
 Labeled each one as **emotion** or **investment.**
 Then cut the emotional buys by half.

In one year, she paid off two credit cards.
 In two years, she had a six-month emergency fund.
 Now? She's buying her first duplex.

She said,

"I stopped using money to escape my life—and started using it to *build* it."

THIS ISN'T ABOUT GUILT. IT'S ABOUT GROWTH.

You're not wrong for wanting comfort.
 You're human. You've been through a lot.
 And sometimes, a little retail therapy *does* feel like medicine.

But don't let comfort rob you of capacity.

The same money you spent to look wealthy could've bought you ownership.
 The same money you used to distract yourself could've funded your freedom.

This isn't about being perfect.
 It's about being **purposeful.**

STRATEGIC INVESTING IS MORE THAN STOCKS

It's time to expand your definition of "investment."

Every dollar can go to one of three things:

- **Consumption** – temporary pleasure
- **Comfort** – emotional relief
- **Creation** – long-term reward

CONTROL THE PULSE

Strategic investing means choosing *creation* more often.

It's investing in:
- Skills
- Tools
- Businesses
- Property
- Experiences that expand your world, not shrink your wallet

And yes—investing in your healing too.

STORY: THE GUY WHO STARTED WITH $10

Andre was broke. But he had a phone. And a library card.

Instead of spending ten bucks on fast food, he bought a book on branding.

Then another on marketing.

Then he started freelancing. Built his portfolio.
Now he runs a small agency.

He said,

"Every dollar I didn't waste became a seed."

The flip wasn't magic. It was a mindset.

Narrator's Reflection:

Money is more than currency. It's commitment.
And every dollar you spend says something about the life you're building—or avoiding.

So ask yourself:
Is this transaction building the person I claim I want to become?

CONTROL THE PULSE

If not, slow down.
 Redirect.
 Invest with intention.

Because when your money moves with purpose, so does your future.

CHAPTER 22

LEARNING THE LANGUAGE OF LOGIC — SPEAKING TRUTH OVER TRIGGERS

"You don't drown in emotion. You drown in the story you keep telling yourself about it." — Tierre Ford

The way you talk to yourself matters.
Not just *what* you say—but *how* you say it... especially when life hits you hard.

Most people don't realize it, but they speak in **triggers**, not truths.

- "I always mess up."
- "Nothing ever works out."
- "This is just who I am."
- "They don't care about me."
- "It's too late to change."

Sound familiar?

That's not logical. That's an emotional *echo.*

It's pain rehearsing itself in your mind—until it becomes your language.

THE WAR OF WORDS INSIDE YOUR HEAD

Your internal dialogue is the script your life follows.
If the script is full of fear, blame, or hopelessness…
Your decisions will follow that tone.

CONTROL THE PULSE

And if your decisions stay emotional, your life stays in reaction mode.

Learning the **language of logic** is how you change that.
It's not about being cold.
It's about being *clear.*

It's how you calm your mind without silencing your soul.

STORY: NINA AND THE JOB THAT BROKE HER

Nina got laid off unexpectedly.

First thing her mind said:

"You're a failure. You're replaceable. You're behind."

That voice was loud.
Louder than the truth.
Louder than her experience.
Louder than all the wins she'd stacked before.

Then her mentor asked her a question:

"Is that the truth—or just your trigger talking?"

That one sentence snapped her out of it.

She paused.
Sat still.
Started rewriting the script.

Instead of: *"I'm behind,"*
She told herself: *"I'm being repositioned."*

That one phrase helped her focus. Apply. Rebuild.
Two months later, she landed a higher-paying remote job with more freedom.

All because she changed the *language inside her head.*

CONTROL THE PULSE

THE MOST DANGEROUS LIES ARE THE ONES YOU REPEAT TO YOURSELF

When you're triggered, your brain scrambles for certainty.
So it grabs whatever's loudest—old fears, childhood wounds, past trauma.

It doesn't ask: *Is this logical?*
It just reacts.

That's why you have to **be louder than the lie.**

Because unchecked thoughts grow roots.
And rooted lies become reality—even when they're false.

REPLACING REACTIONS WITH RATIONAL TRUTH

Start here:

1. Identify the Trigger Phrase

Example: "I'm not good enough."

2. Ask: Who Told Me That? And When?

Track the root. That voice didn't start with you.

3. Replace It With a Grounded Statement

Not fake positivity—but *real truth.*

- "I'm not behind—I'm on my own timeline."
- "I've made mistakes, but I'm still growing."
- "What I feel isn't the full truth."
- "I can pause here without staying stuck here."

This isn't about lying to yourself.
It's about *leading* yourself.

CONTROL THE PULSE

STORY: THE MAN WHO STOPPED ARGUING WITH HIMSELF

Jordan struggled with jealousy.
Every time someone else won, his mind screamed:

"You're losing. You'll never catch up. They're better."

He'd spiral. Overthink. Freeze.

One day, he caught himself mid-thought and asked:

"What if this isn't about them winning...
...what if it's about me not choosing my own race?"

That shifted everything.

He started celebrating wins without comparing.
He used the trigger as a signal to work—not worry.
His language changed.
So did his life.

TRAINING YOUR TONGUE TO SERVE YOUR FUTURE

You don't have to shout positive affirmations all day.
But you do have to *correct the lie* when it shows up.

Speak like someone building something.

- Clear.
- Calm.
- Committed.

This is how you anchor your identity.

Every time you replace a trigger with truth, you give your future a better foundation.

QUICK LOGIC LANGUAGE FRAMEWORK

Use this when your thoughts spiral:

CONTROL THE PULSE

A. What am I feeling right now?
(Name the emotion, don't judge it.)

B. What story am I telling myself about this?
(Be honest. Don't pretty it up.)

C. What's the actual truth—based on facts, not fears?
(Truth always sounds less dramatic but more solid.)

D. What do I want to happen next?
(This focuses your decisions forward, not backward.)

E. What's one small move I can make from this truth, not the trigger?
(That's your power move.)

STORY: HOW A SINGLE SENTENCE SAVED A FRIENDSHIP

Jada almost cut off her best friend after one ignored text.

Her trigger said: *"She doesn't value me."*

But before blocking her, she paused and asked:

"Is this about her... or about how I fear being forgotten?"

She waited.
 Had a conversation instead of a confrontation.

Turns out her friend was dealing with a private family crisis.

One pause.
 One question.
 One shift in language—saved years of friendship.

That's the power of logic over trigger.

Narrator's Reflection:

Your mind will talk.
 The question is—*who's doing the talking?*

CONTROL THE PULSE

If it's the old you, the wounded you, the triggered you…
 The story will never change.

But the moment you speak truth over noise—
 You start living by design, not drama.

And the most powerful people in any room?
 Aren't the loudest.
 They're the ones who've mastered the conversation within.

CHAPTER 23

BUDGETING WITHOUT THE SHAME SPIRAL

"A budget is not a restriction. It's a declaration.
It doesn't say, 'You can't.'
It says, 'This is where I'm going—and here's how I'm getting there.'" — *Tierre Ford*

Let's be real.

Most people hear the word **"budget"** and immediately think:

- Struggle.
- Lack.
- Can't afford.
- "I'm broke."
- "I messed up."

It's a trigger word.
Because somewhere along the way, budgeting became a punishment.
Not a plan.

But here's the truth nobody told you:
Budgeting isn't about guilt. It's about clarity.
It's not a cage—it's a compass.

And when done right, it's not about what you *can't* do.
It's about what you *can finally do.*

CONTROL THE PULSE

THE SHAME SPIRAL LOOKS LIKE THIS

1. You overspend.
2. You feel bad.
3. You avoid looking at the numbers.
4. You stop tracking.
5. You keep spending to "feel better."
6. You feel worse.
7. Repeat.

It becomes a cycle of emotional sabotage.

You know what you *should* do.
 But shame makes you delay.
 Delay makes you drown.

And the longer you avoid your money, the harder it is to trust yourself with it.

STORY: HOW LAMONT ESCAPED THE CYCLE

Lamont made $80K a year—but always felt broke.

He didn't track his spending.
 Didn't want to "feel like a child with an allowance."

Every overdraft fee hit like a slap.
 Every decline at the store triggered a quiet panic.

Then one day, tired of feeling powerless, he sat down with his bank statements and broke down crying.

Not because he was poor—but because he'd been *unaware*.

He wasn't failing—he was just floating.

He built a budget that felt like a mission.
 Month by month, he took his life back.
 He now calls his budget "my map to freedom."

CONTROL THE PULSE

WHY YOU DON'T NEED TO BE PERFECT—JUST PRESENT

Budgeting isn't about becoming a spreadsheet wizard.

It's about facing what's real.

It's saying:

"I may not have it all together—but I'm here. I'm looking. I'm learning."

Most people don't budget because they're bad with money.
They don't budget because they feel bad about money.

Big difference.

REDEFINING THE B-WORD: WHAT A BUDGET REALLY IS

A budget is just a plan for your money to go where *you* tell it to.

Think of it like:

- A GPS for your income
- A fence around your priorities
- A permission slip to spend on what matters

It's not a no—it's a *not now*.
It's not "you're broke"—it's "you're being strategic."

PRACTICAL BUDGETING WITHOUT THE EMOTIONAL BACKLASH

1. Start With Vision, Not Guilt

Don't begin your budget by listing what you "can't buy."
Start by naming what you *want your money to do for you.*

- Pay off debt?
- Travel more?
- Start a business?

CONTROL THE PULSE

- Save for peace of mind?

That's your "why." Your anchor.

2. Track, But Don't Obsess

Use simple tools. Even a notebook works.
The goal isn't perfection—it's awareness.

You can't master what you won't measure.

3. Make It Visual

Budgets shouldn't live in dusty spreadsheets.
Write them on whiteboards. Color-code them. Use visuals.
Make your money journey something you can *see*, not just dread.

4. Celebrate Every Micro-Win

Saved $25 this week? That's a win.
Said no to an impulse buy? That's control.
Gave yourself grace instead of guilt? That's healing.

Small wins build trust—and trust fuels transformation.

STORY: THE SINGLE MOM WHO BUILT HER WAY OUT

Clarissa made $42K a year with two kids.
Budgeting used to feel like grief.
She hated saying no to her children. Hated feeling "less than."

But once she reframed her mindset, everything changed.

She called it her "family wealth plan," not a budget.
Every month she involved her kids. Showed them where the money went.

They celebrated together when they reached their savings goals.

Three years later?
She owns a home. Has a six-month emergency fund.
And her kids think budgeting is *normal.* Empowering.

CONTROL THE PULSE

She said,

"The budget didn't make me smaller. It made me *stronger.*"

GIVE YOURSELF PERMISSION TO BECOME POWERFUL

You don't owe anyone shame for your financial past.
You don't have to carry guilt for what you didn't know.

Budgeting isn't about fixing a broken you.
It's about guiding a powerful you.

And every time you sit down to write your budget, remember:

- You're not poor. You're planning.
- You're not failing. You're forecasting.
- You're not limited. You're *learning to lead.*

Narrator's Reflection:

Most people don't fear budgeting.
They fear what budgeting might reveal.

But what if the numbers weren't there to judge you—just to *guide* you?

What if the shame was never yours to carry in the first place?

Take it off.
Open the notebook.
Write the plan.
And remember: you don't need more money to start—you need more **intention.**

CONTROL THE PULSE

CHAPTER 24

HOW RICH PEOPLE USE NUMBERS, NOT NERVES

"Money doesn't respond to emotion. It responds to math."
— *Tierre Ford*

When rich people make decisions, they don't guess.
They **measure.**

They don't ask:

- "How do I feel about this today?"
  They ask:
- "What do the numbers say?"

While most folks are reacting, hoping, worrying, or wishing...
Wealthy minds are calculating.

They trust numbers more than nerves.
And that one shift?
It's the difference between surviving and scaling.

THE POOR MINDSET IS EMOTIONAL—THE WEALTH MINDSET IS STRUCTURED

Here's how it plays out:

- **Poor mindset:** "I feel like I can afford this."
- **Wealth mindset:** "What's the long-term ROI?"
- **Poor mindset:** "I hope this investment works."
- **Wealth mindset:** "Let's break down the risk-to-reward ratio."
- **Poor mindset:** "I deserve this right now."

CONTROL THE PULSE

- **Wealth mindset:** "Does this align with my 5-year target?"

It's not that rich people don't have emotions.
They just don't *lead with them.*

They let data decide—then move with discipline.

STORY: THE BARBER WHO LEVELED UP

Mike owned a small barbershop in the south side of Houston.
He had hustle, skill, and loyal clients—but still lived check to check.

Why? Because he ran his business off *vibes,* not *figures.*

He didn't track profit. Didn't study foot traffic. Didn't analyze pricing.

One of his clients—a retired CPA—challenged him:

"You are cutting heads, but you are bleeding money.
Know your numbers or stay stuck."

That hit.

Mike started budgeting. Cut unnecessary expenses.
Raised his prices $5. Lost a few clients—but kept the ones that mattered.

He doubled his monthly income in 6 months.

And now?
He trains other barbers in "Math-First Hustling."

Because the numbers don't lie.
Your nerves do.

FEELINGS FLUCTUATE—DATA STANDS STILL

Emotions change with mood, weather, sleep, and stress.

But numbers?

- Don't care how tired you are.

CONTROL THE PULSE

- Don't shift with your mood swings.
- Don't lie to make you feel better.

That's why smart investors, business owners, and decision-makers ask:

- What's the cost?
- What's the revenue?
- What's the time ROI?
- What's the probability?
- What's the risk if this fails?

Emotion says, *"I'm nervous."*
Wealth says, *"Run the math."*

TOOLS RICH PEOPLE USE THAT NOBODY TAUGHT US

1. **Net Worth Tracking**
   They know exactly what they own minus what they owe.

2. **Cost-Benefit Analysis**
   Every big decision runs through this filter:
   Does the benefit outweigh the cost?

3. **Time Valuation**
   They know what one hour of their time is worth—and delegate everything below that number.

4. **Compound Interest Calculators**
   They don't guess how savings grow. They chart it.

5. **Risk Assessment Frameworks**
   If it fails, how bad does it hurt me? If it wins, how much does it move me forward?

STORY: THE SINGLE MOTHER WHO BECAME A LANDLORD

Desiree worked two jobs and raised three kids on her own.
She used to say: "I'm not good with money."

CONTROL THE PULSE

Then one Sunday, she heard a speaker say:

"You don't need to be good with money—you need to be *honest* with it."

That night, she wrote out every expense, every dollar in, every dollar out.
 She didn't cry. She calculated.

She realized she could afford to buy a duplex if she cut the extras and kept her tax refund.

A year later, she moved into one side and rented out the other.
 Her rent covered the mortgage.

Now she owns two more.
 Not because she felt rich—but because she *thought* rich.

SWAP NERVES FOR NUMBERS IN YOUR OWN LIFE

Here's how to start:

1. Don't Decide Big on Bad Days

Nerves are loud when life's noisy.
 If you're tired, anxious, broke, or rushed—pause. Breathe. Wait. Then decide.

2. Ask: "What Would This Look Like on Paper?"

Strip the feeling. Write out the facts.

- What's the actual cost?
- How long till I get ROI?
- What's the best and worst case?

3. Track More Than You Spend

Track your habits. Track your time. Track your energy.
 Wealthy people measure everything. Why?
 Because what gets measured gets managed.

CONTROL THE PULSE

4. Build a 'No Emotion Budget'

Every dollar has a job.
No dollar moves unless the math makes sense.

WHY MOST PEOPLE STAY STUCK IN NERVE MODE

They never learned to slow down.
They make decisions to feel better, not *be* better.

- They buy to fix boredom.
- Quit to fix discomfort.
- Invest based on someone else's excitement—not their own evidence.

Wealthy people move like chess players, not gamblers.

And if the math doesn't add up?
They don't move. Period.

Narrator's Reflection:

Most people were raised to survive, not strategize.
We were taught to *react*, not *review*.

But you can learn.

And when you stop flinching at numbers—and start using them to your advantage—
You unlock a power your emotions could never give you:

Certainty.

Not because everything's guaranteed. But because you've run the math, trusted the data, and built the plan.

That's what rich people do.
And now, that's what *you* do too.

CHAPTER 25

THE ART OF WALKING AWAY FROM A BAD DEAL

"Every time you say yes to the wrong thing, you delay the right one." — *Tierre Ford*

Most people think power is **taking the deal.**
But real power is **turning it down—and still sleeping like a baby.**

Walking away isn't a weakness.
It's **wisdom.**

It means you know your worth.
You trust your plan.
And you don't need desperation disguised as opportunity.

A BAD DEAL ALWAYS COSTS MORE THAN IT PROMISES

It might look good upfront.
It might come dressed in urgency or sparkle.
But the fine print? The silence? The gut feeling?

That's where the truth lives.

Bad deals come with:

- Emotional pressure
- Vague timelines
- Hidden costs
- Imbalanced power
- Long-term headaches disguised as short-term wins

CONTROL THE PULSE

And here's the trick:
They almost always show up *right before* a real breakthrough.

You'll feel it: the tension between "I could…" and "I shouldn't."

That's your cue.

STORY: THE MAN WHO ALMOST SOLD TOO EARLY

Jared had built a small but thriving online store.

A bigger company approached him with a buyout—six figures upfront, but he'd lose all rights to the brand.

He needed the money. His family was behind on bills. His nerves were screaming, *"Take it!"*

But something inside paused.
He remembered what his mentor told him:

"Never sell your baby to someone who sees it as a product."

He walked away.

Two years later, he rebranded, scaled—and sold for **seven figures.**

Walking away wasn't the easy choice.
But it was the one that kept him in control.

KNOW YOUR WALKAWAY POINT—BEFORE YOU NEED IT

Don't decide your standards in the middle of the storm.

Decide *now*.

- What's non-negotiable?
- What does a *bad deal* look like in your world?
- What red flags will you never ignore again?

If you don't define your line, you'll cross it every time emotion gets loud.

CONTROL THE PULSE

WHY PEOPLE STAY IN BAD DEALS (AND BAD RELATIONSHIPS, JOBS, CONTRACTS)

Because they confuse discomfort with destiny.
Because they're addicted to potential.
Because they think walking away means **starting over.**

But here's the truth:
You're not starting over. You're *starting smarter.*

Walking away is often the most strategic move you can make.

STORY: THE WOMAN WHO CHOSE DIGNITY OVER DESPERATION

Sasha was offered a publishing deal for her memoir.

The contract looked shiny—until she read the fine print:

- 70% royalties to the company
- Creative control stripped
- Rights locked for 10 years

Everyone told her to take it.
"This is your chance."
"Exposure matters more than money."

She said no.

Instead, she self-published. Promoted it herself. Built her own lane.

Her book hit bestseller lists in two categories.
And she kept 100% of her freedom—and her profit.

She didn't fold.
She *flourished.*

THE RED FLAGS OF A BAD DEAL (TRUST THESE)

1. **They Rush You**

CONTROL THE PULSE

If someone's pushing you to decide *now*, they're hiding something that can't survive daylight.

2. **They Guilt-Trip You**
   If the deal needs manipulation to move forward, it's already off balance.

3. **They Downplay Your Concerns**
   If "Don't worry about that" is their answer to every question—worry.

4. **They Benefit More Than You**
   If the upside is all theirs and the risk is all yours, it's not a partnership—it's a setup.

PRACTICAL TOOLS TO MASTER THE WALKAWAY MINDSET

1. Create a Deal Filter

Have a written list:

- If it doesn't hit these 3 values, I don't engage.
  This saves you from emotional decisions in the heat of the moment.

2. Train Yourself to Say "Let Me Think About It"

You don't owe anyone an answer on the spot.
Pausing is power.

3. Exit Without Explaining Everything

You don't have to justify protecting your peace.
"No" is a full sentence.
"Not interested" is a strategy.
"Thank you for the offer" is classy. Let that be enough.

4. Keep an Abundance Mindset

There's always another deal.

CONTROL THE PULSE

Scarcity makes people say yes too fast.

WHY WALKING AWAY BUILDS CONFIDENCE

Because it proves something to yourself:

- You can trust your judgment.
- You don't chase validation.
- You value alignment over applause.

And that confidence?
It echoes.

People feel it. Respect it. Gravitate toward it.

You become someone who doesn't just **talk smart**—you *move smart.*

Narrator's Reflection:

Every "no" you say to a bad deal opens the door to a better one.
But you can't receive it if your hands are full holding the wrong thing.

This chapter isn't just about business.
It's about life.
And the lesson is this:

Every deal has a price. The question is—are you paying in peace, purpose, or power?

Walk away if it costs too much.

CHAPTER 26

FROM HUSTLE TO DISCIPLINE: BUILDING TRUE WEALTH

"Hustle might feed you—but discipline will free you."
— *Tierre Ford*

Let's get this straight up front:

Hustle is the spark—not the system.
It's meant to be the beginning, not the lifestyle.

Yes, hustle gets you noticed.
Yes, hustle opens doors.
Yes, hustle helps you escape survival.

But without structure, hustle becomes a prison with a dress code.
And too many people confuse exhaustion with elevation.

True wealth doesn't shout.
It whispers. It multiplies.
It moves in discipline.

THE LIE THEY SOLD YOU ABOUT "GRINDING"

You were told to grind forever.
 That rest is for the weak.
 That working harder means you deserve more.

But here's the truth:
Hard work alone won't make you wealthy.
Systems will.

Discipline is where your hustle turns into equity.
Without it, you're just running faster on the same wheel.

CONTROL THE PULSE

STORY: THE COURIER WHO BURNED OUT AND BOUNCED BACK

Andre was known as the hardest working guy in the room.
Three delivery apps. Six days a week. Fourteen hours a day.
He was making $7,000/month. But had nothing to show for it.

No savings. No rest. No time.

Then came the crash.
Literally. A car wreck.

No vehicle. No income. No protection.

After the pity and panic, he built a new muscle: discipline.
He learned money management. Tracked every dollar. Invested slowly.
Eventually started his own small courier company—this time, with drivers under him.

He works smarter now.
Not because he gave up hustle.
But because he **graduated from it.**

HUSTLE IS REACTIVE. DISCIPLINE IS STRATEGIC.

Hustle says: "I need to work harder."
Discipline says: "I need to work **wiser.**"

Hustle reacts to pressure.
Discipline moves on **purpose.**

Hustle is loud.
Discipline is **predictable.**

You don't need more grind—you need more guidance.

WHAT TRUE WEALTH ACTUALLY LOOKS LIKE

Wealth is not just money.

It's:

CONTROL THE PULSE

– Freedom over your time
– Ownership over your income
– Peace in your daily decisions
– Assets that pay you without begging
– A life that works even when you don't

And you don't build that from energy—you build it from **systems**.

FIVE DISCIPLINE SHIFTS THAT BUILD REAL WEALTH

1. Track before you spend.
Wealthy people know where every dollar is going.
They don't move money off emotion.
They ask, "What's the job of this dollar?"

2. Invest consistently, not emotionally.
Hustlers buy high and panic sell.
Builders stick to the plan—rain or shine.
Consistency beats timing. Every time.

3. Delay gratification, not joy.
You're not depriving yourself. You're teaching yourself.
The new shoes can wait. Your future can't.

4. Automate your systems.
Set it and forget it.
Automatic savings. Auto-investments. Monthly check-ins.
Discipline wins when your life runs on design—not emotion.

5. Protect your energy like it's capital.
Time, focus, peace—those are your **real assets**.
Don't spend them on people or projects that drain you.

STORY: THE NURSE WHO BUILT HER OWN FREEDOM

Kenya was a full-time nurse, deep in debt, drowning in fatigue.
One night after a double shift, she sat in her car and asked herself,
"Is this it?"

CONTROL THE PULSE

She didn't quit her job.
She started investing slowly.
Saved her tax refunds. Bought a duplex. Lived on one side, rented the other.

Ten years later—no more shifts.
She now owns multiple units and runs a real estate mentorship program.
Kenya didn't just escape.
She **transformed**—because she chose discipline over hype.

DISCIPLINE IS THE REAL FLEX

Anyone can grind.
Not everyone can **stick to a system.**

Discipline means:

– No more living check to check
– No more "winging it" financially
– No more burnout disguised as ambition
– No more chasing—just building

Narrator's Reflection:

Hustle saved you.
But now it's time to **outgrow it.**

Because real freedom isn't earned by sweat.
It's earned by **structure.**

Discipline is how you protect your peace.
How you build your future.
How you make sure all that hard work was never in vain.

The grind got you here.
But discipline... discipline is what's gonna take you **further than you ever imagined.**

CHAPTER 27

MONEY ARGUMENTS: WHY COUPLES FIGHT & HOW TO STOP

"It's never just about the money. It's about what the money means." — Tierre Ford

If love is the fire, money is often the fuel.
It can warm you—or burn everything down.

Couples don't fight because one spent $300 at the mall.
They fight because:

– One feels disrespected
– One feels unsafe
– One feels out of control
– One's past trauma is triggered

The argument isn't about the receipt.
It's about the **relationship between money and emotion.**

WHY COUPLES REALLY FIGHT ABOUT MONEY

Because money isn't neutral.

To one partner, money might mean **freedom.**
To the other, it means **security.**
To one, it means **power.**
To the other, it means **survival.**

So when someone spends $1,000 on a luxury item, it might feel like self-love to one—and sabotage to the other.

CONTROL THE PULSE

Same dollar.
Different meanings.
That's the war.

STORY: THE SILENT FIGHTERS

Travis and Mia weren't yelling.
They were doing something worse—**withdrawing.**

Travis believed in saving. Grew up poor. Lived on coupons and scarcity.
Mia believed in enjoying life now. Her parents always said, "You can't take it with you."

Every time Mia booked a trip, Travis would shut down.
Every time Travis brought up budgets, Mia felt controlled.

They weren't fighting over cash.
They were fighting over childhood ghosts.

THE ROOTS OF MONEY TRAUMA IN RELATIONSHIPS

Money wounds come from:

– Watching parents fight about bills
 – Experiencing eviction or food insecurity
 – Being praised or punished based on material things
 – Associating love with gifts—or lack of them

So when you're in a relationship, you're not just splitting expenses. You're merging *histories.*

That's why logic doesn't fix money fights.
Understanding does.

5 REASONS COUPLES CLASH OVER CASH

1. Different Money Stories
One partner sees saving as safety. The other sees spending as

CONTROL THE PULSE

freedom.
Neither is wrong. But unspoken expectations lead to resentment.

2. No Shared Financial Vision
If you're not aiming at the same target, you'll shoot each other instead.
You need one shared plan—or prepare for constant conflict.

3. Power Struggles
When one earns more, it can create an unspoken "who's in charge" vibe.
This leads to secrecy, control, or quiet rebellion.

4. Hidden Debts or Secrets
Financial infidelity is real.
Lying about credit cards, hidden accounts, or unpaid loans breaks trust fast.

5. No Communication System
If you only talk about money *when it's an emergency*, it's always going to be a war.

HOW TO STOP FIGHTING AND START BUILDING

1. Talk About Money *Before* It Becomes a Problem
Don't wait for the fight.
Schedule a "money date" once a month—light food, no pressure, real talk.

Ask each other: – What did money mean to you growing up? – What does financial peace look like to you? – What are we saving for?

2. Create a Judgment-Free Zone
If one person feels judged, they'll shut down.
Make it safe to talk—even when the answers aren't perfect.

3. Build a Plan Together
One person can't be the CFO of the whole relationship.

CONTROL THE PULSE

Sit down. List all income, bills, savings goals, and desires.
Agree on a **joint strategy**—and a **personal allowance** for both of you.

4. Define Roles Based on Strengths
One person might be better at numbers.
The other might be great at planning for the future.

You don't have to split everything 50/50.
You just have to agree on the roles.

5. Protect the Partnership, Not the Ego
You're not enemies.
You're not proving who's smarter.
You're protecting the mission—*together.*

STORY: THE COUPLE WHO TURNED THE FIGHT INTO A PLAN

Jasmine and Will used to fight monthly.
Bills. Spending. Vacations. Savings. Tension.

One night, they decided to flip it.

Instead of fighting over the problem, they attacked the solution.
They created a "Sunday night check-in."
Set goals. Assigned roles. Built a vision board.

Three years later?
– Paid off $72,000 in debt
– Bought their first home
– Still married. Still peaceful.

They say,

"We stopped fighting *each other*—and started fighting *for each other.*"

Narrator's Reflection:

CONTROL THE PULSE

Money fights are rarely about money.
 They're about fear.
 Control.
 Power.
 And unmet expectations.

The cure isn't in more money.
 It's in more **honest.**

If you and your partner can face your stories—
 You can rewrite your future.

Together.

CONTROL THE PULSE

CHAPTER 28

SPENDING TO IMPRESS IS EMOTIONALLY EXPENSIVE

"You'll go broke trying to look rich—and stay empty trying to look full." — *Tierre Ford*

Let's talk about one of the most expensive addictions on Earth:

Approval.

Not drugs. Not jewelry. Not shoes.
But the need to *be seen* a certain way—even if it breaks you to keep it up.

Because when you spend to impress, you're not buying things.
You're renting confidence.
And it expires every time someone else shows up with something newer, flashier, or more expensive.

You're not in competition.
You're in **emotional debt.**

WHY PEOPLE SPEND TO IMPRESS

It's not because they're bad with money.
It's because they're **unhealed.**

We chase designers to hide insecurity.
We chase luxury to escape poverty.
We chase status to avoid being invisible.

But validation is a bottomless pit.
And you'll never fill a void with more stuff.

CONTROL THE PULSE

STORY: THE MAN WHO DRESSED RICH AND DIED BROKE

Reggie had it all—on the outside.
BMW. Rolex. Flights every other week. Bottles. Suits. The works.

But everything was on credit.
He owed the IRS, owed child support, owed the streets.

The truth? He was terrified to look average.
Even more terrified to admit he was faking it.

By the time he hit rock bottom, his car was repossessed, his accounts frozen, and his name—burnt out.

All that money?
Spent trying to impress people who weren't thinking about him after the party ended.

SIGNS YOU'RE SPENDING FOR APPROVAL, NOT PURPOSE

– You feel ashamed when you can't afford something
– You upgrade things that still work just fine
– You feel anxiety if your outfit/car/house doesn't match your peers
– You care more about **how it looks** than **how it fits your life**
– You get defensive when someone questions your financial choices

If you've felt even one of these, it's time to ask:

"Who am I trying to impress—and what am I losing in the process?"

THE TRUE COST OF IMAGE-BASED SPENDING

It costs you:

– **Peace**: You're constantly worried about appearances
– **Progress**: You're too broke to invest in real moves
– **Partnerships**: Real ones leave when they see you're faking it
– **Possibility**: You never get ahead, because your money's stuck in keeping up

CONTROL THE PULSE

The people you're trying to wow?

They don't pay your bills.
They won't show up in your hard times.
And they won't refund your regrets.

STORY: THE WOMAN WHO TOOK BACK HER FINANCIAL POWER

Tanya used to buy something every Friday—handbags, nails, brunch, hair, new fits.
She was praised for looking put together, flawless, "that girl."

But she was behind on her student loans. Her credit card was maxed. And she cried in her car more than anyone knew.

One night, she deleted her shopping apps.
Started tracking her money. Stopped flexing.
Six months later—debt cut in half. Confidence is higher than ever.
Because she finally started dressing for *herself*, not for strangers.

THE SHIFT: FROM SPENDING TO STUNT → TO SPENDING WITH STRATEGY

You're allowed to look good.
You're allowed to treat yourself.

But if it's draining your accounts and your self-worth?
It's not style. It's self-sabotage.

Ask yourself:

1. Can I afford this twice?
If not, it's not in your wealth bracket yet.

2. Is this for me—or for how I'll be perceived?
If it's for them, leave it.

3. Will I still want this in six months?
Impulse is emotional. Legacy is intentional.

CONTROL THE PULSE

REPLACING THE NEED TO IMPRESS WITH INNER STRENGTH

When your self-worth goes up, your need to prove yourself goes down.

You stop needing new things to feel new.
You stop needing applause to feel accomplished.
You stop chasing luxury and start building wealth.

Because real power?
It's quiet.
It's focused.
And it's funded by wisdom—not wounds.

Narrator's Reflection:

There's no peace in pretending.
No freedom in fronting.

Spend for joy, not for show.
Invest in who you're becoming, not who you're trying to impress.

And remember:
The people worth keeping don't need a performance.
They just want you to be real—and rich in peace, not pressure.

CHAPTER 29

YOUR BANK ACCOUNT DOESN'T LOVE YOU BACK

"You love the money. But the money doesn't love you."
— *Tierre Ford*

You check it like it's a text from someone you care about.
You chase it like it owes you loyalty.
You cry over it. Smile for it. Break your back trying to grow it.

But let's make one thing clear:
Your bank account has no emotions.

It doesn't care how hard you worked for the deposit.
It doesn't remember the hours you gave up to make it grow.
It's a reflection of numbers, not love.
Currency, not commitment.

And once you learn that?
You stop worshipping money—and start **wielding it.**

THE MYTH OF "MONEY LOYALTY"

People talk about being loyal to their job, their bank, their grind.
But let's be honest—**money has zero loyalty in return.**

You can give 20 years to a company and get laid off in a meeting.
You can deposit every check, play by every rule, and still be hit with overdraft fees the moment you slip.
You can work a double shift, skip your kids' events, and stay broke by Friday.
Why?

CONTROL THE PULSE

Because **money responds to management—not emotion.**

STORY: THE MAN WHO LOVED THE MONEY TOO MUCH

Darius made six figures.
Designer everything. Picked up every tab. Loaned money out like a hero.

But he never tracked his spending.
Never invested. Never saved.
He thought his *income* made him powerful—until he got laid off.

Suddenly, the money stopped showing up.
And so did all the people who loved what the money did for them.

That was the day he realized—

"I loved my money like it was a person.
But it left me like a stranger."

WHAT MONEY ACTUALLY IS

– It's a **tool**, not a trophy
– It's a **resource**, not a relationship
– It's a **mirror**, not a measure of your soul

Money is neutral. It flows to structure.
It stays where it's respected.
It grows where it's given **purpose**.

Your emotions won't protect your balance.
Your feelings won't build equity.

What will?

Systems. Boundaries. Intentionality. Ownership.

SIGNS YOU'RE ATTACHED TO MONEY THE WRONG WAY

– You panic when the number drops
– You equate your worth with your income

CONTROL THE PULSE

– You feel guilty for saving instead of spending on others
– You think a big paycheck will fix your emptiness
– You call money your "baby"—but treat it like a sidepiece

The result?

Emotional burnout. Financial chaos.
And a constant loop of "Why can't I get ahead?"

HOW TO BUILD A HEALTHY RELATIONSHIP WITH MONEY

1. Name the job of every dollar.
Unassigned money disappears.
Give each dollar a purpose: save, invest, enjoy, give.

2. Separate your value from your vault.
You are not your balance. You are not your debt.
Your humanity is deeper than digits.

3. Treat money like a business partner, not a lover.
Track performance. Assess returns. Make smart, clear moves.

4. Protect your peace more than your points.
No amount of flexing is worth your mental health.

5. Love people. Use money. Not the other way around.

STORY: THE WOMAN WHO FINALLY CHOSE PEACE

Rosa used to chase checks like validation.
More money meant she mattered. Meant she was "winning."

But she was always drained. Always anxious. Always comparing.

One day, she got sick. Had to stop working.
Her bank account dipped—but for the first time, she felt **free**.

She journaled. She breathed. She started learning what money really meant.
She built a new budget. Bought less, but lived more.

CONTROL THE PULSE

Now? She's peaceful, paid, and nobody's puppet.

Narrator's Reflection:

Money is important. But it is not intimate.
It will not hug you back. It will not save your marriage. It will not raise your kids.

It will go where it's told.
And disappear when it's not respected.

So stop begging it to love you.
And start loving yourself enough to **master it.**

Because once you stop chasing money like it's a relationship,
You'll finally start building wealth like it's a legacy.

CHAPTER 30

GET RICH SLOW: THE EMOTIONLESS WEALTH PLAN

"Slow money is grown money. Loud money is lost money."
— *Tierre Ford*

Everybody wants to get rich fast.
But the question you need to ask is:

"Do I want to *feel* rich—or actually *be* rich?"

One is a rush.
The other is a roadmap.

One is emotional—quick wins, risky plays, dopamine hits.
The other is intentional—boring steps, quiet growth, real power.

The truth is, most people don't need to get rich fast.
They just need to stop going broke emotionally.

THE MYTH OF THE FAST TRACK

Social media shows the highlight reels:

– Flashy trades
 – Crypto runs
 – Lottery wins
 – "I turned $500 into $500K overnight" scams

But behind the filters is bankruptcy, burnout, or back to zero.

Here's what the wealthy won't always post:

Real wealth is slow. Quiet. Repeatable. Boring.
And that's what makes it *work*.

CONTROL THE PULSE

STORY: THE "BORING" MAN WHO BECAME A MILLIONAIRE

Harold never bought crypto.
 Never day-traded. Never flipped houses.

He worked a $60K job, saved 30%, invested monthly into index funds.
 Didn't touch it. Didn't flaunt it. Didn't panic when the market dipped.

Thirty years later—multi-millionaire.
 Debt-free. Two homes. Zero stress.

No followers. No flex.

Just a man who played the slow game—and won.

WHY GETTING RICH SLOW WORKS

1. It removes the panic.
 When you have a plan, you stop reacting to every headline or trend.

2. It protects your energy.
 You're not on the emotional rollercoaster of "win big or lose everything."

3. It builds confidence, not just cash.
 Every step you master makes you stronger. Every habit adds up.

4. It's scalable.
 Slow money stacks over time—and starts working harder than you do.

5. It's harder to lose.
 Because you're not gambling. You're building.

THE EMOTIONLESS WEALTH PLAN

Let's keep it clean, simple, and cold-blooded:

CONTROL THE PULSE

1. Automate your savings.
Every time you get paid, your future gets paid first. No decision. No delay.

2. Invest monthly, not emotionally.
Pick your vehicles—index funds, ETFs, IRAs.
Set it. Forget it. Adjust only when your life changes.

3. Avoid hype. Stay in the lane.
Don't chase the "next big thing."
Own the **boring assets** that quietly grow:
– Real estate with long-term tenants
– Dividend stocks
– 401(k) employer matches
– Simple portfolios with compound interest

4. Keep lifestyle creeps on a leash.
More money shouldn't mean more spending.
Lock in your lifestyle. Let the extra grow your empire, not your ego.

5. Revisit the plan once a year. Not once a day.
Wealth isn't built through obsession. It's built through rhythm.

STORY: THE HYPE TRADER VS. THE PLANNER

Jamal made $80,000 trading options in six weeks.
Then lost $90,000 trying to repeat it.

Ashleigh made $500/month investing since she was 23.
Never looked rich. Never move fast.

At 40, Ashleigh owns three rentals and a six-figure portfolio.
Jamal's restarting from scratch—again.

One chased feelings.
The other followed facts.

CONTROL THE PULSE

WHEN YOU MASTER THE SLOW GAME, YOU MASTER YOUR LIFE

You don't need to win the lottery.
You don't need to go viral.
You don't need to prove anything to anybody.

You just need to:

– Know your numbers
– Respect the process
– Stay emotionally out of the way

And trust that **time is your teammate**—if you stop fighting it.

Narrator's Reflection:

Fast riches are loud.
Slow riches are loyal.

Most people don't have a money problem.
They have a **patience problem.**

Get rich slowly.
Sleep well.
Stack forever.

Because in the end, the calmest builder always owns the block.

CONTROL THE PULSE

CHAPTER 31

ATTRACTION VS. ALIGNMENT

"Just because it glows doesn't mean it grows you."
— *Tierre Ford*

Attraction is instant.
 Alignment is intentional.

One makes your heart skip.
 The other makes your life work.

In every area—relationships, business, friendships—we often chase what's *magnetic*, not what's *meant*.
 And we pay for it.

Because attraction is chemistry.
 Alignment is **chemistry plus clarity.**

THE DIFFERENCE THAT COSTS PEOPLE YEARS

Attraction says:

"I want it."

Alignment asks:

"Will it still want me when I evolve?"

Attraction is how it feels today.
 Alignment is how it fits tomorrow.

And most of your pain?
 Comes from calling attraction "destiny"...
 And finding out too late was just a distraction **in disguise.**

CONTROL THE PULSE

STORY: WHEN LOVE WAS LOUD, BUT NEVER LASTING

Tamika was drawn to confidence. To presence. To power.
Every man she dated had "it"—that energy that filled the room.

But they couldn't listen.
Wouldn't grow.
Never stayed long.

They attracted each other like fire and gasoline.
Lit up. Burned out. Every time.

One day, her therapist asked:

"What if you're chasing chemistry with people you're not compatible with?"

Tamika paused.
That was the first time she stopped looking for a spark...
And started looking for **peace**.

ALIGNMENT LOOKS LIKE:

– Values that match when the cameras are off
 – Conversations that sharpen, not just entertain
 – Honesty that doesn't require decoding
 – Growth that doesn't threaten the connection
 – Goals that build, not break, the future

Attraction can bring people in.
Only alignment can **keep** them there.

THIS GOES BEYOND LOVE

This is **money**.
Business.
Friendship.
Faith.
Strategy.

CONTROL THE PULSE

You can be attracted to: – A high-paying job that ruins your health
– A business deal that flashes fast, but lacks integrity
– A partner who fills your bed, but empties your soul
– A "mentor" who inspires you, but doesn't respect you

Attraction pulls.
Alignment **positions.**

QUESTIONS TO ASK YOURSELF:

1. Do our long-term values match—or just our short-term interests?

2. Would I want this connection if it offered no perks or praise?

3. Does this partnership support the person I'm becoming—or keep me tied to who I was?

If the answer isn't clear,
Don't chase chemistry.
Check the *compass.*

STORY: THE BUSINESS DEAL SHE WALKED AWAY FROM

Naima got offered a six-figure deal.
Big brand. Big exposure. Big ego on the other end.

She almost signed—until the terms changed.
They wanted her voice—but not her vision.
Her story—but not her truth.

Her mentor told her:

"You can cash the check now and fight for your soul later…
Or walk now and keep your power intact."

She walked.
Built her own brand.
Made her first million the next year—with her values untouched.

CONTROL THE PULSE

ATTRACTION IS THE TEST. ALIGNMENT IS THE REWARD.

The things that tempt you aren't always trying to *build* you.
Sometimes, they're sent to test if you've learned yet.

To see if you'll:

– Choose peace over praise
– Choose substance over spotlight
– Choose depth over dopamine

Alignment doesn't always look exciting.
But it always feels **safe.**
Whole. Clean. God-approved.

Narrator's Reflection:

Attraction will make you chase.
Alignment will make you rise.

It's not about what draws you in.
It's about what you can *grow within.*

Be bold enough to leave the spark behind—
If it can't handle your fire.

Because when you stop confusing attention for love…
And motion for meaning…
You'll finally align with **everything you deserve.**

CONTROL THE PULSE

CHAPTER 32

HOW TO DATE WITHOUT LOSING YOUR MIND

"You can't lose your mind over someone who hasn't found theirs." — Tierre Ford

Dating in today's world feels like playing chess in a hurricane.
Swipe culture. Ghosting. Trauma-bonding. Oversharing. Undelivering.
One minute it's potential.
The next minute, it's panic.

But here's the truth most people don't say out loud:

Dating doesn't have to break you.
You can protect your peace *and* your heart.
You can love deeply without losing yourself.

But only if you date with your eyes open—and your mind intact.

WHY PEOPLE LOSE THEIR MIND IN LOVE

Because they confuse chemistry with character.
They romanticize potential over patterns.
They date from loneliness, not clarity.

And instead of asking,

"Does this add to my life?"
they ask,
"Do they like me?"

Wrong question.
The right one is:

CONTROL THE PULSE

"Is this person aligned with my future—or just a distraction in my present?"

STORY: SHE LOVED THE IDEA, NOT THE REALITY

Bri was smart. Successful. Healed-ish.

She met Jordan—charming, deep voice, future talk. It was electric. But two months in, he started disappearing. Mood swings. Inconsistencies.
Her friends warned her. Her gut whispered.

But she held onto hope. Why?

Because she fell in love with the version he sold her—not the one he kept showing her.

When it finally ended, she wasn't just heartbroken.
She was angry at *herself* for ignoring the signs she saw clearly from day three.

DATING WITHOUT LOSING YOUR MIND MEANS:

– You're whole before the hello.
You're not auditioning. You're observing.

– You know your non-negotiables.
And you stick to them when it's hard—not just when it's easy.

– You slow down physical intimacy.
Not because you're scared. But because you're serious.

– You take people as they are—not as you imagine them.
You listen with your ears. Not just your hopes.

– You leave when peace leaves.
Even if it looks good on paper. Even if it's been months. Even if you're "invested."

CONTROL THE PULSE

SIGNS YOU'RE DATING FROM WOUNDS, NOT WISDOM

– You're scared they'll leave, even when they treat you poorly
– You ignore red flags because "no one's perfect"
– You feel anxious more than you feel seen
– You try to earn their love with effort instead of letting it be mutual
– You over-explain your boundaries to someone who doesn't value them

Reminder:
If you have to lose yourself to keep them, they were never yours to begin with.

HOW TO DATE WITH PEACE AND POWER

1. Have a vision for your life before you date.
 You can't measure alignment without a map. Know what you want—and what you *won't accept.*

2. Stop chasing vibes. Start checking values.
 Do they handle conflict well? Are they consistent? Do they speak your love language—or just mimic it?

3. Learn to be okay with silence.
 A person who disappears when you set boundaries wasn't built for the journey. Let them go.

4. Heal your need to be chosen.
 When you choose yourself first, you'll never beg again.

5. Ask better questions.
 – "How do you respond to stress?"
 – "What's your relationship with money, family, growth?"
 – "What's your biggest lesson from past relationships?"
It's not just cute convos—it's vetting your future.

CONTROL THE PULSE

STORY: THE MAN WHO DATED WITH INTENTION

Marcus used to chase beauty and chemistry.
 But after two toxic relationships, he started dating differently.

He wrote down his values. Focused on emotional maturity. Watch *actions*, not just words.
 Stopped sleeping with people too fast. Stopped giving second chances to confusion.

He met someone new. She was steady. Smart. Slow-burning.
 Not loud. But real.

They built a friendship first. Healed *in peace*, not pain.
 Two years later, they were building a business—and a home.

Not a fantasy. A future.

Narrator's Reflection:

Dating doesn't have to leave you bleeding.
 It doesn't have to feel like survival.

You are not too much. You are not too picky. You are not unlovable.

You're just learning that love without clarity is chaos.
 And attention without alignment is a trap.

Date with your whole heart—
 But keep your mind sharp.

Because the right one won't cost you your sanity to keep.
 They'll bring peace to your purpose—and add rhythm to your rise.

CONTROL THE PULSE

CHAPTER 33

LUST, LOVE & LIES – EMOTIONAL FILTERS IN ROMANCE

"When lust wears off and lies fall apart, only love stands still." — *Tierre Ford*

You don't see people as they are.

You see them through filters—of your trauma, your hope, your hormones, and your hunger to be wanted.

Romance? It's never just about *them.*

It's about how you *feel* when you're with them.

And that's where we get in trouble.

Because feelings lie.

Lust lies.

Even love—without wisdom—will mislead you.

THE THREE FILTERS THAT FOOL YOU

1. Lust – The Firestarter
It feels urgent. Electric. Addictive.
It makes you skip steps.
It makes bad decisions look good in candlelight.

Lust doesn't ask:

"Can we build a life?"
It asks:
"Can we escape this moment together?"

2. Love – The Illusion of Security
Love makes you hold on, even when peace walks out.

CONTROL THE PULSE

You remember the first month. The laughs. The way they said your name.

But sometimes, the person you love isn't loving *you* anymore.
And what you're calling loyalty is just emotional attachment dressed up as hope.

3. Lies – The Unseen Architect
This one's the hardest.
Because lies aren't always external.
Sometimes you lie *to yourself.*

– "They'll change."
– "It's not that bad."
– "At least I'm not alone."
– "They're just going through something."

No.
They're just showing you the truth—
You're not ready to face it.

STORY: THE FILTER THAT NEARLY BROKE HER

Alyssa met Dev at a conference.
Well-spoken. Suited up. Dreamer. Romantic.

He made her feel like a queen. Fast.
Two weeks in, she said "he could be the one."

But something didn't feel right.
He avoided emotional accountability.
Spent more than he made.
Love-bombed her with gifts but ghosted during conflict.

Her best friend said:

"You're not in love with him.
You're in love with how you felt for five days."

CONTROL THE PULSE

She didn't want to hear it.
 Until one day, he disappeared—with her credit card and her peace of mind.

SIGNS YOU'RE SEEING THROUGH EMOTIONAL FILTERS

– You ignore consistent red flags for occasional green ones
 – You replay the good times to excuse the bad patterns
 – You're addicted to how they *make you feel*—even if it's 80% confusion
 – You stay because of time invested, not value received
 – You keep rewriting the same story, hoping for a different ending

HOW TO UNFILTER YOUR HEART

1. Slow it all the way down.
 If it's real, it won't expire. Take time to see who they are *after* the fireworks fade.

2. Ask hard questions early.
 "What does emotional accountability mean to you?"
 "What do you believe love looks like in conflict?"
 You're not being too deep. You're being intentional.

3. Trust actions. Question patterns.
 One good day doesn't erase months of inconsistency.

4. Keep your logic on the table.
 Date with your heart open, but your brain turned on.

5. Love from overflow—not desperation.
 You are not a rehab center. You're not here to fix someone who won't fix themselves.

STORY: THE MAN WHO WALKED AWAY FROM "LOVE"

Kareem thought he was in love with Janine.
 But after two years of emotional rollercoasters, he realized something painful:

CONTROL THE PULSE

He wasn't in love.
He was trauma-bonded.
Stuck in a loop where chaos felt like chemistry.

It wasn't until he took 90 days to be alone—no dating, no distractions—that he finally felt peace.

When he met someone new, it wasn't a rush.
It was calm. Clarity. Aligned.

Not filtered by fear.
But filled with truth.

Narrator's Reflection:

Lust can be loud.
Love can be blinding.
And lies—especially the ones we tell ourselves—can cost us years.

But when you remove the filters and face people with your whole, healed mind,
You stop falling in love with potential—
And start building with *reality*.

Because in the end, your heart doesn't just need passion.
It needs *peace, purpose, and protection*.

CHAPTER 34

ATTACHMENT STYLES AND FINANCIAL RUIN

"Your money problems might not be math—they might be emotional attachment dressed as survival." — *Tierre Ford*

You learned to love before you learned to count.
You learned to attach before you knew what a budget was.

And if no one told you better—
you're still managing your bank account
with the same survival instincts you used to manage your childhood fears.

The result?

You don't have a spending problem.
You have an *attachment* problem.

And it's silently leaking through your wallet, credit score, and sense of worth.

THE FOUR ATTACHMENT STYLES (AND THEIR FINANCIAL SHADOWS)

1. Anxious Attachment

"If I don't give or spend, I'll lose them."

– Constantly over-giving in relationships
– Buying love, peace, or attention
– Feeling guilty when you save or set financial boundaries
– Avoiding your bank statements like they're bad news

CONTROL THE PULSE

Financial Fallout:
You people-please with your pockets.
You say yes with money when your heart wants to say no.

2. Avoidant Attachment

"I don't need help. I don't trust anyone with my money."

– Hyper-independent
– Refuses to merge accounts or talk openly about finances in relationships
– Sabotages shared goals because they fear control
– Hides purchases or creates separate financial lives

Financial Fallout:
You protect yourself so much, you stop building wealth together.
You confuse secrecy with security.

3. Disorganized Attachment

"I crave closeness but fear it. I want wealth but self-sabotage."

– Wild swings: budget one month, blow it the next
– Uses money to regulate emotional highs and lows
– Constantly jumps between saving and splurging
– May grow up with financial chaos and recreate it in adulthood

Financial Fallout:
You chase the emotional high of control—but feel shame after every impulse move.
You don't trust your financial self.

4. Secure Attachment

"Money is a tool. Love is safe. Boundaries are normal."

– Open and honest about finances
– Can save, invest, and spend in alignment
– Comfortable discussing money with partners
– Doesn't use cash to control or cope

CONTROL THE PULSE

Financial Freedom:
 Money becomes a mirror—not a mask.
 They make decisions based on goals, not fear.

STORY: SHE COULDN'T STOP SAVING HIM

Sierra had her stuff together.
 She had a good job, a 720 credit score, and a real plan.

Then came Trey—charisma in sneakers. Struggling artist. Full of dreams, not receipts.

He needed help. She gave.
 He needed a place. She signed the lease.
 He had another emergency. She paid.

Why?

Because she was *anxiously attached* to the idea of being "enough to make him stay."

She didn't just lose thousands.
 She lost years.
 And the version of herself that knew she deserved better.

EMOTIONAL ATTACHMENT + MONEY = SILENT SABOTAGE

Here's the part they don't teach in school:

You don't earn peace just by working harder.
 You earn peace when you heal your emotional relationship with money.

So ask yourself:

– Do I spend it to prove I'm lovable?
 – Do I save to feel in control of chaos?
 – Do I give too much to feel safe?
 – Do I hide money to protect my wounds?

CONTROL THE PULSE

Every dollar has a story.
What's yours saying?

HEALING STARTS HERE

1. Know your attachment pattern.
Get honest about how you act when you feel threatened, unloved, or uncertain.

2. Separate money from worth.
You're not "better" because you give more—or "less than" because you save more.
Money is math. Emotion makes it messy.

3. Set financial boundaries—even in love.
A real relationship will respect a budget.
You don't have to bleed to be loyal.

4. Learn to sit in the discomfort of "no."
You don't owe anyone your last dime. Or your peace.

5. Seek wholeness—not rescue.
Your money can't fix your abandonment wounds.
Only healing can.

STORY: THE MAN WHO NEVER SHARED HIS ACCOUNTS

Isaiah grew up poor.
When he made six figures, he swore he'd never let anyone "take" from him again.

He kept all his accounts separate—even from his wife.
Made every decision solo. Hid his fears behind control.

Then one day, she left—not for the money, but for the *distance*.

Isaiah realized he'd been saving his money... but losing his intimacy.
It wasn't greed. It was traumatic.
And he had to choose: his fears—or his future.

CONTROL THE PULSE

Narrator's Reflection:

Your heart and your wallet are more connected than you think.
If you don't heal the way you attach—
you'll keep paying for things money can't fix.

This isn't just about finance.
It's about freedom.

Because when your emotions no longer control your money…
you finally start building a life no one can take away.

CONTROL THE PULSE

CHAPTER 35

ARE YOU CHOOSING OR ESCAPING?

"Don't call it a path if it's just a hiding place."

— *Tierre Ford*

There's a line so thin, most never see it until they're deep in debt, deep in drama, or deep in regret.

That line is the difference between choosing something...
 and using it to escape something else.

A job.
 A relationship.
 A move.
 Even healing.

Too many people are calling *coping* "clarity."
 They're calling distractions "decisions."
 And they're running toward something... just to run away from themselves.

ESCAPE LOOKS LIKE CHOICE—UNTIL YOU SLOW DOWN

You think you're in love.
 But really? You're tired of being alone.

You think you want to move.
 But really? You just hate your current self.

CONTROL THE PULSE

You think you need a new job.
But maybe? You're just not facing what's broken inside your discipline.

Escape feels like momentum.
But it's actually a loop.
You start over—again and again—and call it a fresh start.
But it's just a fresh mask.

STORY: THE WOMAN WHO MOVED TO "START OVER"

Tasha left Atlanta for Houston. New city. New job. New energy.

But six months in, it was déjà vu:
Same bad habits. Same financial mess. Same lonely nights.

She realized something painful:
She hadn't moved forward. She just moved *away*.

She didn't need a new city.
She needed a new standard.

And until she changed her inner wiring, her outer world stayed the same—just with different scenery.

HOW TO TELL THE DIFFERENCE

Ask yourself:

1. Am I running *to* something... or running *from* something?
Be honest. One leads to growth. The other just delays pain.

2. Do I feel grounded in this decision—or desperate?
True choices feel solid. Escapes feel like sprints.

3. Is this rooted in clarity or exhaustion?
Big life moves made while tired often lead to more chaos.

4. If no one was watching, would I still choose this?
If the answer is no, it's performance—not purpose.

CONTROL THE PULSE

ESCAPE ALWAYS COMES BACK AROUND

You can change jobs, partners, cities, even hairstyles.
But if your *core self* doesn't grow—your problems pack a bag and come with you.

They'll show up:

– In the next relationship
– In the next bank account
– In the next late-night anxiety spiral

You don't need a bigger blessing.
You need a cleaner why.

STORY: THE MAN WHO STARTED FIVE BUSINESSES

Carlos was smart. Driven. Hustler mindset.

But every time a business hit month six, he burned out.
Switched industries. Rebranded. Blamed the market.

It wasn't the business. It was his belief:

"If I just stay moving, I'll never have to face my fear of failing."

What he called ambition was actually avoidance.
He wasn't building. He was *hiding behind the grind.*

It took stillness for him to finally succeed.

CHOOSING MEANS:

– You've asked the hard questions
– You're not afraid of discomfort
– You're willing to say no, even if it looks good
– You act with intention—not reaction
– You know what you're moving toward—and why

ESCAPING LOOKS LIKE:

– Rushing decisions without a real plan

CONTROL THE PULSE

– Using work, love, or change to numb pain
 – Avoiding mirrors, feedback, or accountability
 – Confusing busy with productive
 – Constant rebranding with no real transformation

Narrator's Reflection:

The world tells you to chase.
 But sometimes the strongest move is to sit still and ask yourself:

"Why am I really doing this?"

When you choose with clarity,
 You build a life that can weather storms.
 When you escape out of fear,
 You build a sandcastle with no foundation.

You owe it to yourself to know the difference.

Because every decision you make from fear
 will cost your future self peace.

Choose wisely.
 Choose consciously.
 And above all—choose you.

CONTROL THE PULSE

CHAPTER 36

HIGH-VALUE LOVE REQUIRES HIGH-VALUE THINKING

"If your mind ain't expensive, your love won't be either."
— *Tierre Ford*

Everybody wants high-value love.
But not everyone is thinking at that level.

They want loyalty—without logic.
They want royalty—while still reasoning from wounds.
They want "forever"—without asking themselves if they're even built for *clarity*.

Let's make it plain:

You cannot build a high-value relationship with low-value thinking.
Not in 2025. Not in any year.

WHAT DOES "HIGH-VALUE THINKING" REALLY MEAN?

It's not about money.
It's about *mental discipline.*
It's about the emotional maturity to step back before stepping in.

It means asking the hard questions, like:

– "Is this love or attachment?"
 – "Is this connection or a convenient distraction?"
 – "Am I choosing this person—or trying to fix them?"
 – "Can we grow together, or are we just vibing on delay?"

CONTROL THE PULSE

High-value thinking puts purpose above panic.
Clarity over chemistry.
Principles over pressure.

STORY: THE MAN WHO "LOVED" BUT NEVER LED

Reggie was known as a good guy.
Flowers, trips, Instagram captions. He looked the part.

But emotionally, he coasted.
He had no vision.
No plan.
No structure to support the kind of woman he kept praying for.

He dated women with discipline—but brought *vibes instead of vision*.

Eventually, they left—not because they didn't care, but because they were tired of holding up a house built with empty words.

HIGH-VALUE LOVE IS BUILT ON:

1. Communication that's direct, not dramatic.
No guessing games. No silent treatment. If it's love, it's honest.

2. Emotional accountability.
You own your triggers. You don't bleed on someone who didn't cut you.

3. Mutual elevation.
You challenge each other. Spiritually. Financially. Mentally.

4. Clear expectations.
No "go with the flow" after six months. Purpose brings plans.

5. Standards that don't collapse under loneliness.
You don't lower the bar just to avoid being alone.

LOW-VALUE THINKING SOUNDS LIKE:

CONTROL THE PULSE

– "They have potential."
– "At least they don't cheat."
– "I'll just see where it goes."
– "I can't ask for too much."

Every time you think like that,
 you're telling your future self:

"I'm okay settling for less than I prayed for."

STORY: THE WOMAN WHO DECIDED TO LEVEL UP— ALONE

Maya dated men who were "almost."
 Almost ready.
 Almost consistent.
 Almost enough.

One day, she looked in the mirror and asked:

"What would the *healed version of me* choose?"

That question changed everything.
 She cut ties.
 Did the inner work.
 Got therapy. Studied relationships. Raised her financial game.

And when she finally met someone, she didn't shrink.

Because she wasn't asking to be loved.
 She was choosing to build love—with someone already whole.

HIGH-VALUE LOVE IS NOT A FAIRYTALE

It's a strategy.
 It's emotional discipline.
 It's mutual effort and real vision.

If your brain can't handle tough conversations,
 your heart won't survive a real connection.

CONTROL THE PULSE

If your values can't hold up under pressure,
your loyalty will be bought by vibes.

QUESTIONS TO ASK BEFORE CALLING IT LOVE

– What are our shared goals?
– Can we grow wealth together—or are we just spending?
– How do we fight? How do we recover?
– Are they solution-oriented—or just smooth talkers?
– Do I feel peace or just passion?

Love is a lifetime investment.
Don't make it with a short-term mindset.

Narrator's Reflection:

Your love life is only as evolved as your mindset.
Your peace, your power, your purpose—they deserve partners, not projects.

High-value love isn't about how they look.
It's about how they think, how they lead, how they heal, and how they hold space for both your ambition and your softness.

Don't chase relationships that your *mind* hasn't approved.

Because if your thinking isn't wealthy—
your love will always be bankrupt

CONTROL THE PULSE

CHAPTER 37

STANDARDS OVER EMOTIONS IN RELATIONSHIPS

"Love can feel right and still be wrong. That's why standards save lives." — *Tierre Ford*

You feel it.
The butterflies. The spark. The magnetism.

But let me ask you a harder question:

Do you feel safe? Do you feel seen? Do you feel stable?

Because emotions are loud.
But standards? Standards are quiet discipline.

They're not sexy like late-night texts.
They don't give you goosebumps like a good kisser.
But they protect your future from becoming a cautionary tale.

WHAT HAPPENS WHEN EMOTION LEADS, AND STANDARDS FOLLOW?

You fall fast.
You excuse red flags.
You start calling compromise "maturity."
You say, "They're not perfect" while hiding the fact that they're actually *dangerous* to your peace.

You stay longer than you should.
You settle deeper than you thought.
And by the time your standards wake up, your soul is exhausted.

CONTROL THE PULSE

STORY: THE WOMAN WHO STAYED TOO LONG

Janelle met Marcus at a rooftop party.
Charming. Confidence. The whole package.

Three months in, he never wanted to talk about commitment.
Six months in, he started disappearing for weekends.
Nine months in, she was paying his half of the rent.

But she kept saying:

"We've come too far. He just needs time."

No.
What he needed was boundaries.
And what she needed was to remember her standards—before her self-respect expired.

EMOTIONS ARE VALID.
BUT STANDARDS ARE VITAL.

Feelings tell you what you *want.*
Standards tell you what you *deserve.*

And if your feelings are stronger than your standards,
you will keep choosing chemistry over character—
and calling it "love."

WHAT DO STANDARDS LOOK LIKE IN ACTION?

1. They're clear before connection.
Don't wait until you're "in love" to figure out your non-negotiables.
Write them down. Stand on them.

2. They don't move based on loneliness.
Being alone is hard.
But rebuilding your soul after being broken by the wrong person? That's harder.

CONTROL THE PULSE

3. They speak louder than an apology.
A hundred "I'm sorrys" don't matter if the behavior doesn't change.

4. They protect your peace like a vault.
No one, and I mean no one, should have access to your soft heart without proof they can protect it.

5. They grow with you.
As you level up, so should your standards. If your mind is evolving, your relationships should too.

STORY: THE MAN WHO RESET HIS BAR

David used to date for validation.
If she was pretty and laughed at his jokes, that was enough.

But heartbreak taught him something pain never forgets—

"Your life reflects what you tolerate."

So he rewired.
He started asking better questions.
He stopped ignoring that sick feeling in his gut.

He stopped confusing *potential* with *partnership*.

And when the right woman came, he didn't flinch.
Because this time, his standards had been leading.

QUESTIONS TO AUDIT YOUR RELATIONSHIP STANDARD

– Does this person bring out the healthiest version of me?
– Are our values aligned—or just our hobbies?
– Can I be emotionally honest with them without being punished?
– Are we building something—or just passing time?
– Am I loving them… or managing them?

Standards are not walls. They're filters.
They don't block love—they protect it.

CONTROL THE PULSE

Because real love doesn't ask you to shrink.
 It asks you to rise.

Narrator's Reflection:

Emotion is a beautiful servant—but a terrible master.
 And in love, it'll blind you if your standards aren't wearing glasses.

Feelings come and go.
 But peace? Peace stays when you choose wisely.

So before you say, "I love them,"
 Ask yourself:

"Do my standards love this version of them too?"

If the answer is no,
 it's not time to fall deeper.
 It's time to walk smarter.

CONTROL THE PULSE

CHAPTER 38

ARGUING WITH LOGIC — HOW TO FIGHT FAIR

"If you lose your mind during every disagreement, don't be surprised when peace stops showing up." — *Tierre Ford*

Fighting isn't the problem.
Fighting dirty is.

You can love someone and still get mad.
You can care deeply and still disagree.
That's not weakness—that's *realness*.

But when the gloves come off and logic disappears,
what you're building starts to bleed.

Because disrespect doesn't just bruise egos.
It bankrupts trust.
And in any relationship—personal, professional, romantic—trust is the currency.

EMOTIONS VS. LOGIC IN A FIGHT

Let's break it down.

Emotion says:
"You always do this!"
"I can't believe you!"
"You never listen!"
"Whatever. I'm done."

Logic says:
"When you raised your voice, I felt dismissed."

CONTROL THE PULSE

"I need us to agree on a solution."
"I'm not trying to win—I'm trying to understand."
"Let's take a pause and revisit this calmly."

See the difference?

One escalates.
 The other *elevates.*

STORY: THE COUPLE WHO GOT LOUD BEFORE THEY GOT SMART

Corey and Nia loved each other hard—but fought even harder.

One night, a small disagreement about spending turned into a yelling match.
 No one heard the actual issue.
 Just blame. Sarcasm. Door slams.

Then Nia's friend asked her something that stopped her cold:

"Do you want to be right—or do you want to be understood?"

It hit.

From that moment on, they didn't just learn to talk.
 They learned to fight fair—with *logic, not ego.*

It saved their love.

THE RULES OF FIGHTING FAIR

1. Don't argue to win. Argue to resolve.
 A relationship isn't a courtroom. No one should be on trial.
 You're not enemies. You're teammates in a tense moment.

2. Use "I feel" instead of "You always."
 Attack the problem, not the person.
 The second it gets personal, logic leaves the room.

CONTROL THE PULSE

3. Pause before you punch (verbally or emotionally).
A 10-second silence can save a 10-year relationship.
Don't react—*respond.*

4. Listen to hear, not to reload.
If you're only waiting for your turn to speak, you're not fighting fair.
You're just performing.

5. Clarify the goal.
What's the win here?
Peace? Understanding? Growth?
If it's just "being right," you've already lost.

STORY: THE BUSINESS PARTNERS WHO STOPPED SCREAMING

Malik and Jordan started a media company together.
But once money came in, tensions rose.

Every disagreement turned into a war.
Petty insults. Cold shoulders. Passive aggression.

Their mentor sat them down and said:

"Every fight y'all have takes ten points off your reputation.
So either learn how to talk like men—or get ready to go broke."

That hit was different.

They started writing things out.
Using logic.
Clarifying expectations.
And their profits tripled.

Why?
Because communication is currency.

CONTROL THE PULSE

CHECKLIST BEFORE ANY ARGUMENT

✓ Do I know what I really feel?
✓ Am I calm enough to say it without causing damage?
✓ Have I taken a breath, or am I about to throw blame?
✓ Is this the right time to talk—or do we need space first?
✓ What solution would actually satisfy both sides?

TRAPS TO AVOID

⊘ Scorekeeping.
"This is just like last time!"
(If you forgive it, leave it buried.)

⊘ Character attacks.
"You're just selfish!"
(Stick to the issue—not their identity.)

⊘ Silent punishment.
Ghosting during conflict is emotional immaturity in disguise.

⊘ Bringing in outsiders.
Don't weaponize friends or family. Keep your circle out of your cycle.

Narrator's Reflection:

Conflict will always test your maturity.
It's easy to be sweet when it's sunny.
But love, business, friendships—they're all proven in the *thunderstorms*.

When you fight with logic,
you protect the relationship—even when it's hard.
You create space for growth instead of drama.

So next time tension rises, ask yourself:

"Do I want peace... or pride?"

CONTROL THE PULSE

Because the sharpest minds aren't the ones that never argue—
They're the ones that know *how* to argue without burning everything down.

CONTROL THE PULSE

CHAPTER 39

WALKING AWAY WITH DIGNITY, NOT DRAMA

"The loudest exit is usually covering the weakest healing."
— *Tierre Ford*

Sometimes the most powerful thing you can do isn't fight.

It's a walk away.
 Not with a bang. Not with a post.
 Not with a thread full of shade and screenshots.

But with your head high.
 Your soul is clean.
 And your peace is still intact.

WHEN STAYING BECOMES SELF-BETRAYAL

There's a moment—a quiet one—when you realize:

"This isn't growing me anymore. It's draining me."

And that moment is sacred.

Not because it means you're giving up.
 But because it means you're finally choosing yourself.

Letting go isn't failure.
 Staying stuck in something that's killing your clarity is.

STORY: THE EXIT THAT SAVED HER FUTURE

Tania was engaged to a man who looked perfect on paper.

Big job. Charismatic. Everyone loved them together.

CONTROL THE PULSE

But every time she brought up deeper goals—family vision, finances, faith—he brushed her off.

The ring sparkled. But the respect didn't.

One night, no yelling, no tears, no begging.
She just whispered to herself,

"I love me too much to explain my value again."

She left. No announcement. Just alignment.

And for the first time in years—she slept in peace.

DRAMA IS A DISTRACTION. DIGNITY IS A DECISION.

Let's make it plain.

Drama wants an audience.
Dignity walks out the side door without clapping.

Drama needs validation.
Dignity doesn't need to be understood to feel whole.

Drama is reactive.
Dignity is strategic.

When you walk away with dignity, you don't erase what you gave.
You just stop giving to what no longer grows you.

THE COST OF A LOUD EXIT

You may "win" the argument.
Get likes. Get sympathy.
Even get revenge.

But did you get your peace?

Because the person who walks away yelling isn't healed.
They're still performing for attention.
Still bleeding from places they haven't cleaned.

CONTROL THE PULSE

Dignity doesn't perform.
 It just *moves*.

STORY: THE MAN WHO LEFT THE BLOCK BEHIND

Troy used to run the streets.
 Fast money. Fast women. Fast pain.

One day, after another funeral and another betrayal, he didn't make a speech.
 He didn't threaten to come back harder.

He just packed his bag, turned off his phone, and disappeared into a new version of himself.

No flex. No press release.
 Just healing.

Today, he owns two businesses.
 And not a single person from his old world can say, "He folded."

Because real power isn't about making noise.
 It's about making peace.

HOW TO WALK AWAY WITH DIGNITY

1. Don't explain what they're committed to misunderstanding.
 They'll spin your truth into their comfort zone. Let them.

2. Don't drag others into your exit.
 Your peace doesn't need a hype man.

3. Forgive for *you*, not them.
 Carrying bitterness means they still own a piece of your energy.

4. Focus forward.
 Let go of the story where they play the villain.
 You're writing new chapters now.

5. Move in silence. Elevate in clarity.
 Let your next season be your loudest statement.

CONTROL THE PULSE

QUESTIONS TO CHECK YOUR EXIT ENERGY

– Am I trying to heal… or trying to hurt them back?
 – Would I still be making this choice if no one knew?
 – Does my next step honor my growth—or feed my ego?
 – What version of me is walking out: the triggered one or the wise one?

Narrator's Reflection:

Leaving is hard.
 But sometimes staying is a slow death by self-neglect.

The most dangerous thing isn't walking away.
 It's losing *yourself* while trying to stay loyal to something that isn't.

So walk with your power.
 Leave with your peace.
 Let your silence speak the final truth.

Because real ones don't slam the door.
 They just disappear into their higher calling.

CHAPTER 40

DON'T BUILD A LIFE WITH SOMEONE WHO SPENDS EMOTIONALLY

"If they spend emotions like money with no budget, they'll bankrupt your peace." — *Tierre Ford*

You don't build a kingdom on quicksand.
And you don't build a life with someone whose emotions swing like a wrecking ball.

One day, they're all in.
Next, they're burning bridges and blaming you for the smoke.

They spend emotionally—like it costs them nothing.
But you?
You're the one paying for the overdraft fees with your sleep, your spirit, your sanity.

EMOTIONAL SPENDING IS A SILENT KILLER

It's not always loud.

It looks like:

– Buying gifts after every argument instead of dealing with the root.
– Starting drama just to feel passion.
– Overreacting to small issues and underreacting to real ones.
– Saying "I love you" today and threatening to leave tomorrow.
– Needing chaos just to feel alive.

That's not love. That's an addiction to stimulation.

CONTROL THE PULSE

And if you don't call it out,
 you'll get used to it.
 You'll start believing instability is normal.
 You'll confuse high highs and low lows with depth.

STORY: THE WOMAN WHO BOUGHT HER OWN PEACE

Kendra was dating a man who loved big—but lived wild.
 Every month, a new financial mess.
 Every week, a new emotional explosion.

She kept covering for him.
 Forgiving him.
 Thinking she was being "ride or die."

Until one day, after a public meltdown at a wedding, she realized:

"I've been buying love on credit.
 And now I'm in emotional debt."

She didn't scream.
 She didn't cry.
 She moved out—and moved up.

IF THEY CAN'T MANAGE THEIR EMOTIONS, THEY CAN'T MANAGE A FUTURE WITH YOU.

You're not just building a relationship.
 You're building a *life*.

That means:

– Budgets.
 – Plans.
 – Goals.
 – Conversations that don't end in yelling.
 – Conflict that gets solved, not escalated.
 – Vision that doesn't collapse under ego.

CONTROL THE PULSE

If they can't handle their emotions,
they'll sabotage everything you're trying to build.

EMOTIONAL SPENDING LOOKS LIKE:

– Guilt-tripping instead of communicating.
 – Over-sharing and then weaponizing it later.
 – Acting out instead of speaking up.
 – Storming off, then acting like nothing happened.
 – Apologizing without adjusting.

It's emotional immaturity in designer clothes.
It *feels* intense—but it's hollow underneath.

STORY: THE COUPLE WHO CHOSE GROWTH OVER FIREWORKS

Julius and Brie were passionate—*too* passionate.

Their love life was a movie.
But every week, it turned into a war film.

Until they hit a breaking point:
Missed rent. Burnt friendships. Therapy on the line.

They made a decision:
No more emotional overdrafts.

They learned to pause.
To name feelings.
To budget their energy.

The result?

More peace. More love. Less drama.
Maturity replaced madness.

RED FLAGS OF AN EMOTIONAL SPENDER

▶ Needs chaos to feel connection.

CONTROL THE PULSE

- Can't hold space for disagreement without breaking down.
- Uses affection as currency.
- Treats peace like it's boring.
- Has no emotional savings—every trigger is a full-blown crisis.

SIGNS YOU'RE BUILDING WITH A STABLE PARTNER

- They can disagree without disrespect.
- They self-regulate without shutting down.
- They communicate needs instead of exploding.
- They protect peace like it's gold.
- They understand: emotional maturity is the foundation of long-term love.

Narrator's Reflection:

Love shouldn't feel like surviving a storm every week.
You weren't built to hold someone's chaos with your bare hands.
You were built to *build*.

With someone whose peace matches your purpose.
Whose emotions add fuel—not fire.
Whose presence doesn't just excite you—but *elevates* you.

Because when they spend their emotions like a fool,
you'll end up bankrupt in a relationship you paid everything to maintain.

Choose wisely.
The life you want depends on it.

CHAPTER 41

DON'T LET COMFORT KILL YOU
Part 5: Health Without the Hype

"A slow death wrapped in convenience still ends the same."
— *Tierre Ford*

Let's talk about the real silent killer.

Not cancer.
Not diabetes.
Not even high blood pressure.

Comfort.

That soft, seductive voice that says:

"You've earned the right to relax."
"You'll start next week."
"This isn't hurting anybody."

But it is.
It's killing your stamina.
Your mental edge.
Your willpower.
And eventually… your body.

COMFORT IS A TRAP DISGUISED AS A REWARD

It starts with:

– Skipping a workout here and there.
– Ordering takeout for the third night in a row.

CONTROL THE PULSE

– Telling yourself walking to the fridge counts as cardio.
– Sleeping in late because "you deserve it."

But over time?

You stop running for your life.
And start *sitting in your slow death.*

Your body doesn't lie.
It tells you—quietly, at first.

Breathing heavier.
Thinking slower.
Needing caffeine just to feel normal.
Tired at 3 PM.
Sore from doing *nothing*.

STORY: THE MAN WHO COULDN'T GET UP

Raymond used to be a machine.
Strong. Sharp. Built like confidence.

But in his 40s, business boomed, money came fast—and so did the weight.
He bought the cars, the couches, and the comfort.

One day, his daughter asked him to race her across the yard.

He laughed.
Tried.

And collapsed halfway.

His knees failed. His breath vanished.
His spirit broke in silence.

That night, he didn't cry.
He *counted*—every decision that led him there.

He started walking the next morning.
Now, he runs 3 miles before sunrise.

CONTROL THE PULSE

Because comfort had almost killed him.

COMFORT ISN'T EVIL.
IT'S JUST DANGEROUS WHEN IT'S CONSTANT.

Rest is needed.
But routine laziness does not rest. It's rusty.

We weren't made to *coast.*
We were made to *climb.*

And your health?
It doesn't respond to motivation.
It responds to movement.

SIGNS COMFORT IS KILLING YOU

– You always say "tomorrow."
– You avoid the doctor, the gym, and the mirror.
– You reward yourself with food more than fuel.
– You laugh off your decline like it's normal.
– You don't move unless it's absolutely necessary.

That's not freedom.
That's physical procrastination.

And trust me:
You don't want your body to send you a final notice.

STORY: THE WOMAN WHO WALKED OUT OF THE PIT

Desiree was 310 pounds and 32 years old.
No judgment. Just facts.

One night, after another fast food binge and a brutal panic attack, she whispered to her reflection:

"I'm too young to feel this old."

CONTROL THE PULSE

She started walking the stairs.
Then the block.
Then the treadmill.

It wasn't pretty.
It wasn't Instagram-worthy.
But it was *real*.

Two years later, she wasn't just smaller—
She was sharper. Stronger. Unapologetically awake.

She traded comfort for commitment.
And it saved her life.

WAYS TO ESCAPE THE COMFORT TRAP

1. Move daily—even if it's 15 minutes.
You don't need a gym. You need consistency.

2. Eat like you love your future self.
Not perfect. Just better.

3. Schedule discomfort.
Wake up early. Stretch longer. Fast occasionally. Get uncomfortable on purpose.

4. Track your habits like your money.
What gets measured, gets mastered.

5. Make your environment work for you.
Put the junk food far away. Put the running shoes near. Set yourself up to win.

Narrator's Reflection:

Comfort is the new cigarette.
It feels harmless—until it isn't.

The couch you choose today becomes the hospital bed you fear tomorrow.

CONTROL THE PULSE

The food that makes you "feel good" now becomes the reason you don't feel good later.

You don't have to suffer.
But you do have to sweat.
Just a little. Every day.

Because your body is the vehicle for your vision.
And if the engine fails… the dream dies too.

Let me know when you're ready to take that next breath forward.

CHAPTER 42

EMOTIONAL EATING, LAZY THINKING

"Most people aren't feeding their hunger—they're feeding their feelings." — Tierre Ford

Let's tell the truth most won't say:
The food you reach for during stress is rarely about hunger.
It's about escape.

And the more you eat emotionally,
the more you start thinking emotionally.

It's a cycle.
A quiet one.
But deadly just the same.

FOOD IS FUEL.

BUT TO SOME, IT'S A FIX.

Not for nutrients.
But for numbness.

– That extra slice of pizza after the breakup?
– The candy bag during anxiety?
– The soda "just to get through the day"?

You weren't feeding your stomach.
You were feeding your mood.

And just like that, emotional eating becomes emotional *coping*.

STORY: THE SNACK THAT SPOKE LOUDER THAN WORDS

CONTROL THE PULSE

Loren was a high-performing executive.
 Suited. Scheduled. Sharp.

But every night around 9 PM, she'd crush three bags of chips and a pint of ice cream.

Her therapist asked her one question:
 "What feeling are you trying to quiet at night?"

That question hit harder than any crunch.

Turns out, the food wasn't about flavor.
 It was about loneliness.
 Guilt. Exhaustion.
 The cost of high achievement with no peace.

She didn't need a diet.
 She needed awareness.

LAZY THINKING FOLLOWS EMOTIONAL EATING

The pattern is simple:

You eat heavy, you think heavy.
 Your gut slows, your brain fogs.
 You crave comfort, not clarity.

Why?

Because processed food numbs your nervous system.
 It makes your body lazy—and your thoughts follow.

That's why decisions made in emotional eating spirals often look like:

– "Forget the gym, I'll go tomorrow."
 – "Let me binge-watch instead of build."
 – "What's the point anyway?"

This isn't about shame.
 It's about ownership.

CONTROL THE PULSE

THE LIES FOOD TELLS YOU WHEN YOU'RE IN YOUR FEELINGS

– "This will make you feel better."
– "You deserve this."
– "Just one more won't hurt."
– "You've already messed up—might as well go all the way."

Every bite isn't just calories.
It's a *conversation* between your habits and your healing.

STORY: THE MAN WHO ATE HIS STRESS—UNTIL HE COULDN'T

Kevin had been "the big guy" all his life.
Loved by everyone. Life of the party. But alone with himself? Miserable.

His emotional outlet wasn't women, money, or drugs.
It was food.

Every fight, every doubt, every disappointment—he swallowed it with fries and shakes.

Until one morning he woke up with chest pain and blurry vision.

Doctors said: *Pre-diabetic. Blood pressure is sky-high. Liver inflamed.*

He changed that week.
Not just his meals.
But his *mindset*.

And the man who once needed sugar to survive?
Now runs three wellness groups a month—helping others do the same.

REPLACING EMOTIONAL EATING WITH POWER MOVES

1. Journal before you eat emotionally.

CONTROL THE PULSE

Ask: "What am I really feeling?"
Sometimes it's not hunger—it's fear. Frustration. Boredom. Hurt.

2. Walk before you reach.
 Give yourself 15 minutes of movement.
 Let the emotion pass *through* instead of stuffing it down.

3. Hydrate first.
 Drink water. A lot of emotions show up as cravings when you're just dehydrated.

4. Eat real food, not fake comfort.
 Whole foods regulate mood.
 Processed foods manipulate it.

5. Get uncomfortable in better ways.
 Discipline is its own reward. So is breathing through the storm without using food as a crutch.

SIGNS YOU'RE USING FOOD FOR FEELINGS, NOT FUEL

– You "reward" yourself with junk after hard days
 – You hide food habits from others
 – You eat when bored, angry, or anxious—even when full
 – You mentally crash after certain meals
 – You feel guilt instead of nourishment after eating

Narrator's Reflection:

You don't have a food problem.
 You have a *feeling* problem that food is pretending to fix.

This isn't about losing weight.
 It's about gaining control.

Control over the urge.
 Control over the narrative.
 Control over the energy you carry into your day, your body, your future.

CONTROL THE PULSE

Because lazy eating leads to lazy thinking.
 And lazy thinking leads to stagnant living.

So feed your body like your goals depend on it.
 Because they do.

CHAPTER 43

CUTTING TOXIC PEOPLE WITHOUT GUILT
Part 5: Health Without the Hype

"You weren't born to be someone's emotional landfill."
— *Tierre Ford*

Some people don't want peace.
They just want a place to dump their poison.

And for too long, that place has been you.

It starts small:

– The backhanded compliments.
– The subtle shade when you win.
– The draining phone calls that leave you feeling worse, not better.

Then it grows:

– Guilt-tripping when you set boundaries.
– Undermining your healing.
– Keeping score every time you try to evolve.

It's not just toxic.
It's emotional vandalism.

GUILT IS THEIR FAVORITE TOOL

Toxic people don't always scream.
Sometimes, they sigh loud enough to shame you.

CONTROL THE PULSE

"Wow… you've changed."
"Oh, you're too good for us now?"
"After all I've done for you…"

That's not love. That's *leverage*.

And if you're not careful, guilt becomes your leash.

STORY: THE FRIEND WHO ONLY CALLED TO BLEED

James had a boy he'd known since middle school—Dez.
Same block. Same grind. Same pain.

But while James started reading, building, and growing… Dez stayed in survival mode.

Every call from Dez became a vent session:
Women. Bills. Street drama. Jealous shots.

Never a "How are you?"
Never a "Congrats."
Only complaints. Only chaos.

James stayed loyal—until one day, after a big business win, Dez said:

"Don't forget who was there before you had anything."

That's when James knew:

"You weren't there for *me*. You were there for access."

He changed his number.
No post. No goodbye.
Just *peace*.

NOT EVERYBODY DESERVES FRONT-ROW SEATS TO YOUR EVOLUTION

Let's be clear:

CONTROL THE PULSE

You can love people *from afar.*
You can forgive people *without reconnecting.*

You're not responsible for their healing.
You're responsible for your *boundaries.*

If someone: – Constantly drains you,
– Manipulates you,
– Makes you question your growth,

Then they're not your "day one."
They're your anchor.

And you weren't built to drown.

SIGNS IT'S TIME TO CUT THEM OFF

– You feel anxiety when their name pops up
– They only call when they want or need something
– They minimize your growth
– You feel emotionally exhausted after talking to them
– They guilt you into staying connected

That's not love.
That's dependency in disguise.

STORY: THE COUSIN WHO NEVER GREW UP

Shawna loved her cousin Kenya—they grew up like sisters.

But Kenya always had something negative to say:

– "You think you're better now."
– "That man is gonna leave you like the last one."
– "Everybody fake when they get money."

It hurt. But it *opened Shawna's eyes.*

She started responding less.
Stopped explaining her peace.
Eventually... she stopped picking up altogether.

CONTROL THE PULSE

Kenya's drama kept spiraling.
 Shawna's peace kept rising.

And for the first time, her smile didn't feel borrowed.

HOW TO CUT TOXIC PEOPLE *WITHOUT GUILT*

1. Silence is closure.
 You don't owe an exit interview to people who disrespected your peace.

2. Don't negotiate your boundary.
 The second you explain "why," they try to twist it.

3. Bless and block.
 Pray for them if that's your thing. But cut access.

4. Remember: loyalty has limits.
 You're not disloyal for outgrowing who they refused to become.

5. Replace guilt with gratitude.
 You're not walking away *from* something.
 You're walking *toward* your next chapter.

Narrator's Reflection:

Your peace is sacred.
 So stop handing it out like coupons to people who never paid full price for your presence.

Cutting someone off doesn't mean you're heartless.
 It means you finally have a healthy heart.

You weren't built to carry guilt and greatness at the same time.

So let it go.
 Let them go.
 And walk like your future deserves it.

CONTROL THE PULSE

CHAPTER 44

MOTIVATION IS OVERRATED—DISCIPLINE WINS

Part 5: Health Without the Hype

"Motivation is loud, but it doesn't last. Discipline whispers—and wins." — *Tierre Ford*

Everybody loves motivation.

It's sexy.
It's viral.
It's that goosebump moment in a 60-second clip telling you to chase your dreams at 4 A.M.

But here's the truth they don't post:

Motivation will fail you the moment life gets inconvenient.

Rainy days.
Breakups.
No applause.
Nobody is watching.

That's when motivation disappears—
and the real ones keep going.

Not because they're hyped…
but because they're trained.

MOTIVATION GETS YOU STARTED.
DISCIPLINE KEEPS YOU FINISHED.

Motivation says: *"I feel like it."*
Discipline says: *"It's on the schedule—so it's done."*

CONTROL THE PULSE

Motivation is a mood.
Discipline is a *muscle*.

You can scroll all the quotes you want.
If you don't act without emotion,
you'll keep starting over every Monday.

STORY: THE GUY WHO WAITED FOR "THE RIGHT TIME"

Devonte always talked big.

He had the ideas.
He had the vision.
He even had the perfect playlist to "get in the zone."

But every day, it was something:

– "I'm just not in the headspace."
– "I'll go harder next week."
– "I need to feel it to do it right."

Fast-forward 5 years?
Still talking.

Meanwhile, his quiet friend Jason never said much—
but woke up at 5, worked on his body, wrote that book, built the fund, launched the business.

Jason didn't wait to feel right.
He *just did the work.*

Now Devonte reposts his wins.

DISCIPLINE IS WHAT YOU DO AFTER THE HYPE WEARS OFF

You don't need to be inspired.
You need to be consistent.

Because one day, your feelings will lie to you.
They'll say:

CONTROL THE PULSE

"You've done enough."
"You don't need to show up today."
"Nobody's watching."

And that's when your training kicks in.

SIGNS YOU'RE DEPENDENT ON MOTIVATION

– You can't start unless something excites you
– You ghost your goals when life gets boring
– You start strong but rarely finish
– You binge-watch "grind" content but don't take action
– You crave applause more than progress

Motivation isn't evil—it's just not enough.

STORY: THE WOMAN WHO BUILT WITHOUT FEELING IT

Maria wasn't in the mood to work out.
Or budget.
Or write.

But she made a rule:

"I don't break promises to myself."

So every day, whether tired, sad, annoyed, or unmotivated—she showed up.

Some days, 5 minutes.
Some days, fire.
But always something.

A year later, she didn't just hit her goals.
She became the type of woman who doesn't fold under pressure.

Why?

Because she stopped waiting to feel it—and learned how to be it.

CONTROL THE PULSE

BUILDING DISCIPLINE: THE REAL BLUEPRINT

1. Make it non-negotiable.
 Don't ask, "Do I feel like it?" Ask, "What time does it start?"

2. Stack it with habits.
 Tie new actions to old ones. Stretch after brushing teeth. Budget after payday.

3. Lower the bar, raise the floor.
 If you can't do the full 60 minutes, do 10. Discipline doesn't need perfection—it needs consistency.

4. Measure what matters.
 Track your progress. Small wins build big discipline.

5. Create a system, not a vibe.
 Feelings change. Systems don't.

Narrator's Reflection:

Motivation may sell books, shirts, and TED talks.
 But it won't save you on the days your soul feels quiet.

Discipline will.

Because every great body, bank account, relationship, and legacy wasn't built in a moment of hype.

It was built in moments of silence, sweat, and showing up anyway.

And in this life—
 The quiet doers always outrun the loud dreamers.

CHAPTER 45

HOW TO MAKE DATA-DRIVEN HEALTH CHOICES

"Feelings are loud. But facts know the way."
— *Tierre Ford*

Health isn't a vibe.
It's a system.

And while society sells you meal plans and miracle teas...
data tells you what's really working.

Your body speaks in numbers.
But too many people are only listening to opinions.

They say:

"This worked for my cousin."
"I saw this online."
"This *feels* healthy."

But do you know your own stats?
Or are you gambling with your health because of someone else's hype?

THE DIFFERENCE BETWEEN HYPE HEALTH AND HARD TRUTH

Hype Health:
– 5-day detoxes
– Influencer workouts
– One-size-fits-all meal plans
– "Trust the process" with no benchmarks
– Decisions based on fear, not function

CONTROL THE PULSE

Hard Truth:
- Blood work
- Resting heart rate
- Body fat vs. weight
- Gut microbiome feedback
- Long-term sustainability over short-term drama

This ain't about what's popular.
It's about what's *personal.*

STORY: THE MAN WHO "LOOKED" HEALTHY—UNTIL HE CHECKED

Donnie was lean. Lifted weights. No junk food.
Everyone said he looked *great.*

But he never went to the doctor.

At 36, he finally did.
Cholesterol? Through the roof.
Inflammation? Off the charts.
Blood pressure? High and climbing.

Donnie didn't need a diet—
He needed data.

Now?
Quarterly labs. Daily tracking. Nighttime routines.
And a new rule:

"If I can't measure it, I won't guess it."

TRACKING MAKES YOU HONEST

Think you're sleeping well?
Wear a sleep tracker.

Think you're eating clean?
Log your meals for 10 days straight—no shortcuts.

CONTROL THE PULSE

Do you think your workouts are effective?
Test your strength every 60 days.

Data doesn't lie.
Your ego does.

HEALTH METRICS YOU *SHOULD* BE TRACKING

✅ Resting Heart Rate (RHR)
Tells you how hard your heart is working when calm. Lower is usually better.

✅ Heart Rate Variability (HRV)
Measures how well your body handles stress. Higher = better recovery.

✅ Blood Pressure
Silent killer. Check it regularly—especially if you're stressed.

✅ Glucose Levels
Spikes and crashes affect mood, focus, and fat storage.

✅ Sleep Quality
It's not just hours—it's cycles, depth, and consistency.

✅ Daily Movement
Steps. Active minutes. Mobility range. Movement is medicine.

STORY: THE WOMAN WHO STOPPED FOLLOWING THE CROWD

Kendra tried keto. Then vegan. Then fasting.
Each time, her energy tanked.

Finally, she did a full panel blood test.
Turns out:
– She was anemic
– Low in B12
– Sensitivity to soy and gluten

CONTROL THE PULSE

She wasn't lazy.
She wasn't broken.
She was *uninformed.*

Now she eats for her blood, trains for her recovery, and builds her day around her *actual* needs.

Not TikTok trends.

HOW TO START MAKING DATA-DRIVEN HEALTH DECISIONS

1. Get your baseline.
Book a full-body checkup. Blood work. Hormones. Vitals. Don't guess.

2. Choose metrics that matter.
Pick 3-5 numbers that tie to your goals (ex: blood sugar, sleep, heart rate, weight).

3. Track weekly, not obsessively.
Too much tracking causes stress. Just enough to build *power.*

4. Adjust based on patterns, not feelings.
One bad night isn't failure. Look at trends. Is it getting better? Worse? Staying flat?

5. Use tech—but stay human.
Trackers are tools, not truth. Combine data with how your body *feels*—not just what a screen says.

Narrator's Reflection:

The body is a high-performance machine.
But most people treat it like a mystery box.

They trust how they *feel*—then get blindsided by what they didn't measure.

That ends now.

CONTROL THE PULSE

You don't need to become a biohacker.
You just need to pay attention to your own numbers.

Because one good data point is worth more than 100 emotional decisions.
And the healthiest people in the room?

They don't guess.
They track.
They test.
They *know*.

CHAPTER 46

WHY MENTAL HEALTH REQUIRES MENTAL WORK
Part 5: Health Without the Hype

"You can't journal your way out of what you won't challenge in your mind." — *Tierre Ford*

We treat mental health like a vibe.

Burn some sage.
Buy a crystal.
Post a quote.
Download a meditation app.

But real mental health?

It's not vibes.
It's not trendy.
It's *work*.

And the hardest part?
It happens *inside*—where nobody can see you grinding.

MENTAL HEALTH ISN'T A MOOD—IT'S A PRACTICE

Mental health is like brushing your teeth.
You don't wait until everything rots.

You do it *daily*, even when nothing feels "wrong."
You show up with intention.

Because the mind, like a muscle, weakens without resistance.

CONTROL THE PULSE

And if you don't train it—
the world will twist it.

STORY: THE MAN WHO LOOKED TOUGH BUT WAS BREAKING INSIDE

Lamar was the strong one.
Built like a linebacker. Always calm. Always "good."

Until one night he had a full-blown panic attack in his garage.
It felt like a heart attack. Couldn't breathe. Though he was dying.

It wasn't a weakness.
It was neglect.

No self-checks.
No boundaries.
No space to process trauma.
Just years of bottling pressure behind a smile.

He didn't need a break.
He needed *reconstruction.*

Now? Weekly therapy. Daily walks. Nightly journaling.
He doesn't wait until he's broken to work on staying whole.

THE MYTH: "STRONG PEOPLE DON'T STRUGGLE"

False.

Strong people do struggle.
But they struggle *strategically.*

They ask for help.
They slow down when needed.
They build inner systems before life breaks the outer ones.

Mental health isn't soft.
It's a strategy.

CONTROL THE PULSE

SIGNS YOU'RE AVOIDING THE WORK

– You stay busy to avoid silence
 – You minimize your own trauma
 – You pretend rest is laziness
 – You wear "strong" like a mask
 – You feel guilty for feeling anything at all

That's not strength.
That's *emotional neglect with a smile on top.*

STORY: THE WOMAN WHO NEVER LET HERSELF CRY

Rae grew up hearing:

"Crying is weak."
"Keep your head up."
"Nobody cares about your feelings."

So she didn't cry.
She didn't speak up.
She just kept going—until she couldn't anymore.

At 29, she burned out.
Lost her job, her appetite, her sleep, and herself.

A friend gave her a number for a therapist.
She hesitated. Then called.

It changed everything.

Now? She journals. Meditates. Speaks her truth. Knows her limits.
And *finally* feels safe in her own head.

MENTAL HEALTH WORK THAT ACTUALLY HELPS

1. Therapy or coaching
 No, it's not "crazy." It's clarity.

2. Mindfulness practice
 5 minutes of stillness a day. That's it. No music. Just presence.

CONTROL THE PULSE

3. Thought journaling
Not just writing about your day. Writing about your *thoughts*.

4. Boundaries as self-care
Saying no. Logging off. Cutting noise.

5. Sleep hygiene
Mental health starts at bedtime. Cut screens. Honor the wind-down.

6. Self-talk auditing
Listen to how you speak to yourself. Would you let anyone else talk to you like that?

Narrator's Reflection:

Mental health isn't a quote you post.
It's a system you live in.

You can't fix your mind with surface-level tools.
You have to go deep. Challenge the stories. Dissect the lies.
Sit with the pain—and then *build* from it.

You don't heal just by surviving.
You heal by *understanding what broke*—and choosing not to live there anymore.

And in a world that rewards distraction...
discipline is peace.

CHAPTER 47

FEEL GOOD? DOESN'T MEAN IT'S GOOD FOR YOU
Part 5: Health Without the Hype

"Some of the sweetest poison comes disguised as comfort."
— *Tierre Ford*

We live in a "feel-good first" society.

Comfort food.
Comfort zones.
Comfort love.
Comfort lies.

It's everywhere. You see it on commercials: *"You deserve this."*
You hear it in conversations: *"Do what feels right."*
You follow it without thinking, because who wants to feel bad?

But here's what nobody says out loud:

The most destructive decisions in your life didn't *feel bad* in the moment.
They felt good. Familiar. Easy.

That's what makes them dangerous.

COMFORT IS THE MOST ADDICTIVE DRUG YOU NEVER CHECK FOR

Ask around.

Most people didn't go broke overnight—they spent it to feel better.
Most people didn't lose their health instantly—they ate to self-soothe.

CONTROL THE PULSE

Most people didn't ruin relationships on purpose—they chased the *rush*, ignored the *red flags*.

Feeling good became the goal.
And in chasing it... they lost control.

STORY: THE NIGHT THAT TASTED GOOD BUT TOOK TOO MUCH

DeShawn had been "clean eating" for a month.
Feeling better. Focused. Sharp.

Then came the night out—just one cheat.
Burger, fries, milkshake, wings.

Laughed all night. It felt amazing.

The next morning? Bloated. Groggy. Cravings lit up.
That one night spiraled into two weeks of bingeing.

"It felt good... until I couldn't stop."

That wasn't food.
That was a trigger wrapped in taste.

WHAT FEELS GOOD AIN'T ALWAYS BUILT FOR YOUR FUTURE

Here's what most won't tell you:

– It felt good to stay in that relationship even though it cost your peace.
 – It felt good to overspend even though it broke your budget.
 – It felt good to skip the gym until your back pain returned.
 – It felt good to say yes when you *needed* to say no.

But was it good *for* you?

That's the real test.

CONTROL THE PULSE

HOW TO TELL IF "FEEL GOOD" IS ACTUALLY "FAKE GOOD"

Ask these five questions:
1. Will this decision still serve me tomorrow?
2. If nobody saw me do this, would I still do it?
3. Does this bring relief—or actual healing?
4. What is this replacing that I don't want to face?
5. Would my future self thank me—or resent me?

The difference between winners and wasters?
Winners ask better questions—*before* they act.

STORY: THE LOVE THAT LIT HER UP—AND BROKE HER DOWN

Imani knew he wasn't right for her.

Inconsistent. Possessive. Loud with affection, silent with truth.

But it felt good.
To be wanted.
To be touched.
To be "chosen."

So she stayed.
And she shrank.

Lost her ambition.
Missed her therapy appointments.
Gave more than she ever received.

Until one night, she stood in the mirror, mascara running, and whispered:

"This feels like love… but it's costing my soul."

She walked out. For the last time.

CONTROL THE PULSE

It didn't feel good at first.
But peace rarely does—*until it fully arrives.*

WHEN FEEL-GOOD IS REALLY JUST EMOTIONAL DOPAMINE

Let's call it what it is:

- Doomscrolling = avoidance.
- Emotional eating = sedation.
- Toxic love = validation addiction.
- Compulsive spending = self-worth leakage.

None of it is about the thing itself.

It's about the emptiness *underneath* it.

THE SHIFT: FROM PLEASURE TO POWER

Here's how to flip it:

1. Build new reward systems.
 Make the *right* thing feel good. A cold shower. A deep breath. A hard workout. A budget hit.

2. Interrupt automatic habits.
 Before you react, *pause.* Just 10 seconds. Break the loop.

3. Rewire your "treat."
 Your new version of "I deserve this" = clarity, space, rest, boundaries, progress.

4. Audit your feel-good triggers.
 Make a list. Track how you feel *after*, not just during. Let that data shape your choices.

5. Practice choosing what's good for you—even when it feels boring.

CONTROL THE PULSE

Boring builds empires. Consistency creates confidence. Pleasure fades—*progress doesn't.*

Narrator's Reflection:

Every regret in your life probably came wrapped in a feel-good moment.

That's not a weakness.
 That's wiring.

But wiring can be rewired.

You're not here to be comfortable.
 You're here to be clear.

Because once you learn to separate what *feels* good...
 from what *is* good for you...

you stop chasing cheap highs—
 and start building a life that actually holds up.

No glitter. No gimmicks.
 Just the truth. Peace. Legacy.

CHAPTER 48

STOP JUSTIFYING YOUR VICES
Health Without the Hype

"A bad habit wrapped in a good excuse is still poison."
— *Tierre Ford*

We all have something.

The drink.
The scroll.
The argument.
The late-night craving.
The thing we say we "need" but *know* is slowly killing us.

The problem isn't the vice.
It's how we justify it.

"I had a hard day."
"It's just this once."
"I could be doing worse."
"I've been good lately—I deserve it."

Sound familiar?

That's not honesty.
That's a high-functioning escape plan.

VICE ≠ VICTIMHOOD

There's a difference between self-awareness and self-pity.

CONTROL THE PULSE

One helps you grow.
The other helps you stay stuck.

When you know something is hurting your health, your focus, your relationships, your spirit—and you do it anyway, over and over?

That's not a struggle.
That's self-betrayal in slow motion.

STORY: THE MAN WHO DRANK FOR "STRESS"

Andre was sharp. Suited up. Respectable.
Two kids, a corporate job, mortgage paid.

But every night, after work—two drinks. Sometimes three.

"It takes the edge off," he'd say.
"I'm just relaxing."

Until one night, his daughter found him passed out with the stove still on.

He got lucky. Nothing burned. No one was hurt. But the truth burned deep:

"My stress didn't almost kill my family. My coping did."

He went cold turkey. Not because he was an alcoholic.
But because he was *addicted to escape*.

HOW WE DRESS UP DYSFUNCTION

Let's break the script:

– Junk food becomes "self-care"
– Toxic relationships become "I'm loyal"
– Avoidance becomes "protecting my peace"
– Laziness becomes "just being gentle with myself"
– Porn or endless social scrolling becomes "I'm decompressing"

Let's be real:

CONTROL THE PULSE

If it costs your energy, your time, your purpose, your peace, or your dignity—
it's not helping.

Even if it's trending.

STORY: THE WOMAN WHO CALLED IT "LOVE"

Marina kept going back to him.
The sweet talk. The apologies. The cycle.

Her friends were tired of warning her. She stopped listening.

"He's just broken."
"He had a rough childhood."
"I can help him heal."

But every time she chose to "understand" him, she *betrayed* herself.

The day she finally walked away, she said something that cracked the room:

"I wasn't loving him. I was addicted to *being needed.*"

SIGNS YOU'RE JUSTIFYING A VICE INSTEAD OF HEALING A WOUND

– You get defensive when someone brings it up
– You always have a reason why it's not that bad
– You hide how often you do it
– You feel guilt afterward—but keep doing it
– You only stop when something *forces* you to

That's not balanced.
That's bondage.

HOW TO FLIP THE SCRIPT

1. Stop labeling your triggers as personality traits.
"I'm just a night owl" isn't a reason to binge Netflix at 3AM.
"I'm just emotional" isn't a reason to lash out.

CONTROL THE PULSE

2. Ask: "What am I numbing?"
 Every vice numbs something. Find the source. Fix *that*.

3. Replace—not remove.
 You don't break vices with willpower. You replace them with *rituals*.
 Trade scrolling for journaling. Trade wine for a walk. Trade arguments for breathwork.

4. Track the *cost*.
 Keep a log: time lost, money wasted, energy drained. Let your eyes see what your heart's been denying.

5. Forgive yourself—then hold yourself accountable.
 Guilt changes nothing. Ownership does. You're not bad. You're *ready to stop lying to yourself.*

Narrator's Reflection:

Every vice wears a mask: convenience, comfort, culture, "coping."

But when you strip it down, it's always this:

A deal you made with pain... that pain keeps winning.

You don't need another excuse.
 You need a strategy.
 A standard.
 A higher version of you that says:

"This isn't who I'm becoming."

Because freedom isn't just quitting the habit.
 It's killing the *story* that lets you keep it alive.

And once you stop justifying what's killing you...
 you start *building what saves you.*

CONTROL THE PULSE

CHAPTER 49

INVESTING IN HEALTH LIKE IT'S A BUSINESS

"If your body were a business, would it still be profitable—or bankrupt?" — *Tierre Ford*

You protect your money.
 You track your bank balance.
 You check your credit score.
 You read contracts, calculate ROI, build strategy.

So why don't you do that with your health?

Think about it.

Your body is your longest investment.
 Your mind is your original headquarters.
 Your energy is your operating capital.
 And your habits? That's your business model.

If you're grinding for wealth while running your body into the ground—
 you're not a boss. You're burning the blueprint.

MOST PEOPLE SPEND THEIR 30s CHASING MONEY ...AND THEIR 50s SPENDING IT ON MEDICINE.

Wealth is nothing if you're too sick to enjoy it.
 Love means nothing if your mood is wrecked by diet and sleep.
 Purpose means nothing if your energy runs out by noon.

You don't just get healthy.
 You invest in it.

And like all smart investments, it requires:

CONTROL THE PULSE

- Upfront cost
- Consistency
- Long-term mindset
- Risk management
- Discipline

STORY: THE MAN WHO OUT-EARNED HIS OWN BODY

Derrick had four businesses. Made six figures in two.
But he never slept.
Ate fast.
Lived on caffeine and adrenaline.

"I'll rest when I'm rich," he'd say.

At 42, he had his first panic attack. Then another.
The doctor told him: "Your engine's running like a car that skipped every oil change."

He laughed—until he couldn't.

Now? He tracks meals like invoices.
Trains daily like morning meetings.
And takes recovery days like business off-sites.

"I don't hustle for the grave anymore. I hustle to stay above it."

5 WAYS TO TREAT YOUR *HEALTH LIKE A BUSINESS*

1. Create a "Health Operating Budget."
Time, money, and mental bandwidth. How much are you investing weekly into food, sleep, movement, and rest? If it's zero—you're already in debt.

2. Track Performance KPIs.
Not weight. Not aesthetics.
Real Key Performance Indicators:
- Energy when you wake up
- Mood consistency

CONTROL THE PULSE

- Strength gains
- Focus span
- Inflammation, digestion, sleep quality

These tell the truth before your mirror does.

3. Build Systems, Not Goals.
A goal says, "I want to lose 10 pounds."
A system says, "I lift 3x a week, meal prep Sunday, walk every night."

Systems build sustainable ROI. Goals just burn out.

4. Audit Your Habits Like Expenses.
What are your energy leaks?
Late-night sugar? Netflix till 2AM? Weekend benders?
If it wouldn't pass in your business—it shouldn't pass in your body.

5. Get an Advisor.
Even billionaires use coaches. You don't have to guess your way to wellness. Trainer, therapist, dietitian, accountability partner. Build your health board of directors.

HEALTH IS YOUR FIRST STARTUP

Your mind is the founder.
Your body is the product.
Your habits are the operations.
Your lifestyle is marketing.
And your outcomes? That's the profit.

So the next time you say, "I can't afford to eat clean,"
ask yourself:
Can you afford another hospital bill?
Another day of brain fog?
Another missed moment with your kids because you're too tired to show up?

CONTROL THE PULSE

This isn't vanity.
 This is valuation.

Narrator's Reflection:

People think "investing" means stocks and real estate.
 But the first investment—the one everything else depends on—is the one in the mirror.

If your health crashes, your empire follows.
 If your body breaks down, your dreams slow down.

So take your health personally.
 Run it like a CEO runs their company.

Be disciplined.
 Be strategic.
 Be proactive.

Because nothing compounds faster than a body in motion, a mind in focus, and a soul at peace.

CHAPTER 50

BECOMING THE CALM IN EVERY STORM
Part 5: Health Without the Hype

"Storms don't drown people—panic does." — *Tierre Ford*

Some people walk into chaos—and bring more of it.
Others walk in—and everything starts to slow down.

You've seen it.

A business crisis hits. Everyone scrambles.
Except for one person. They lean back. They breathe. They move with precision.
They become the eye of the storm.

That's not luck.
That's emotional discipline.
And it's one of the highest forms of power you'll ever develop.

CHAOS ISN'T THE ENEMY—REACTIVITY IS

Life will storm.
People will panic.
Plans will unravel.
Your name will be tested.
And emotions will tempt you to match the madness.

But here's the truth:

Calm people don't ignore the fire.
They just don't *become* it.

They let others burn while they build.

CONTROL THE PULSE

STORY: THE ROOM THAT FROZE, EXCEPT FOR HER

At a boardroom meeting, news broke: funding pulled, deals crumbling, media leak.

People stood. Cursed. Argued.
Except her.

Marisol, the quiet one. The least dramatic.
She didn't flinch. She reached for her pen and wrote three moves.

Then she stood and said:

"We don't need a hero. We need a decision."

She outlined a pivot. A phone call. A press reply.
Everyone calmed.
They followed her voice—not because she yelled, but because she *didn't*.

5 HABITS OF THE STORM-PROOF MIND

1. Don't take things personal—take them seriously.
That comment wasn't about your soul. It was about their fear. Learn to separate ego from urgency.

2. Slow your breathing before your reaction.
You can't think while gasping. Before you speak, solve, or respond—inhale. Exhale. Stabilize your body.

3. Focus on the next *controllable* move.
Panic spirals because people zoom out too far. Storm-calmed thinkers zoom in. "What can I do *now* that shifts the odds?"

4. Don't match energy—master yours.
Let others vent, explode, blame. You *observe*. You keep your tempo. Leadership is *emotional tempo control*.

5. Use "if/then" calm conditioning.
Train your brain before chaos. "If they yell, then I pause." "If the deal breaks, then I reassess." Calm isn't just natural—it's trained.

CONTROL THE PULSE

STORY: THE MAN WHO LOST IT ALL—AND STILL SMILED

Kareem was hit from all sides.
Job cut. Breakup. Health scare. Car repo'd.

His cousin asked, "Why are you not mad?"

He said:

"Because I already cried once. Now I'm moving with purpose."

He didn't pretend it didn't hurt.
He just decided pain didn't get to run the show.

"The world can hit me. But I still choose *how I land.*"

HOW TO TRAIN FOR THE STORMS BEFORE THEY COME

- Wake up before the world does. Give yourself quiet before the chaos.
- Do hard things when it's easy. Cold showers. Long walks. Stretch the discomfort muscle.
- Visualize pressure. Play out tough conversations in your mind. Breathe through them.
- Journal your reactions. Every night: "Where did I react emotionally today? What would calm have done instead?"
- Surround yourself with people who don't panic. Panic is contagious. So is peace.

Narrator's Reflection:

Life doesn't promise calm.
It promises storms.

So stop waiting for things to get easier.
Start building the version of you that doesn't shatter when they don't.

CONTROL THE PULSE

Because in every room of noise, power belongs to the quietest soul.
 The one who listens while others yell.
 Think while others react.
 Moves with poise, even when nothing makes sense.

Let the world crash.
 You?
 You'll stay grounded.

Not because the wind stopped blowing—
 But because you learned how to anchor yourself.

Final Thought:

You've made it through 50 chapters of realignment, ownership, and emotional discipline.
 This isn't the end—it's the beginning of you choosing *strategy over sensitivity, power over panic,* and *legacy over reaction.*

Let's build a life that works.
 Not the one that just feels good.

You're not fragile. You're just unfinished.
 Now go finish what the old version of you was too emotional to build.

🔥 THE 5-YEAR LIFE DOMINANCE PLAN

"Discipline across the board—health, money, and love—is the real flex." — *Tierre Ford*

◆ YEAR 1: FOUNDATION – Fix What You've Been Avoiding

HEALTH

- Cut processed food, sugar addictions, and midnight coping habits
- Establish a basic fitness routine (3x per week minimum)
- Begin therapy or solo journaling for mental hygiene

CONTROL THE PULSE

- Sleep and water: monitored, scheduled, respected

WEALTH

- Track every dollar (Budgeting = Truth)
- Eliminate unnecessary monthly expenses and debts
- Start a high-yield savings account or emergency fund
- Learn one wealth skill (investing, trading, real estate, etc.)

RELATIONSHIPS

- Audit current relationships: cut dead weight, remove toxic ties
- Stop dating for entertainment—date for alignment
- Create relationship boundaries and standards list
- Learn your attachment style and emotional triggers

- **YEAR 2: STRUCTURE – Replace Emotion with Framework**

HEALTH

- Follow a disciplined eating schedule and meal plan
- Master one physical discipline: strength training, yoga, or endurance sport
- Build morning/night rituals to reset nervous system
- Remove one destructive vice (cigarette, porn, binge eating, etc.)

WEALTH

- Start investing monthly (ETFs, stocks, crypto, or real estate)
- Increase income through skill stacking or side hustle
- Get financially organized: credit repair, taxes, insurance

CONTROL THE PULSE

- Read 6 books on money, mindset, or business

RELATIONSHIPS

- Practice conscious communication and conflict resolution
- Attract high-value partners/friends by becoming one
- Avoid emotionally expensive relationships—walk early
- Keep a private life. Build a public legacy.

◆ **YEAR 3: GROWTH – Move With Intention or Don't Move At All**

HEALTH

- Track macros, performance, and biometric feedback
- Build a recovery plan: massage, meditation, stretching, supplements
- Train your energy and emotions like a CEO—not a survivor
- Host or lead a local health challenge or community event

WEALTH

- Own or partner in a business venture
- Start passive income streams (e.g., digital product, rental, dividend portfolio)
- Maximize tax write-offs and business structure
- Mentor or coach someone to pass knowledge forward

RELATIONSHIPS

- Choose your tribe: no more lonely hustling
- Deepen 1–2 legacy-level relationships (romantic or platonic)

CONTROL THE PULSE

- Create family wealth habits: money convos, shared visions, real transparency
- Lead with boundaries, not fear

◆ YEAR 4: DOMINANCE – Protect What You Built

HEALTH

- Treat your health like an investment portfolio
- Preventative health checkups, nutritionist, hormone panels
- Build and share a wellness system for your community or family
- Say no to stress that costs your joy

WEALTH

- Scale your wealth with systems: automation, delegation, scaling income
- Become the bank: lend, invest, or fund others with structure
- Own assets: land, businesses, stocks, time
- Build or fund a scholarship, foundation, or investment fund

RELATIONSHIPS

- Partner up or lock in legacy partnerships
- Build wealth with your partner—not just emotions
- Travel with purpose: healing retreats, couple's goal-setting, culture exposure
- Practice grace without losing your standards

◆ YEAR 5: LEGACY – Move Like It's Bigger Than You

CONTROL THE PULSE

HEALTH

- Teach health practices to your kids, mentees, and followers
- Build a personal "life manual": what keeps you whole, sharp, and sane
- Protect your peace at all costs—no matter the relationship, offer, or pressure
- Be the calm in storms for others

WEALTH

- Make your money make money
- Buy time and freedom—then *give it away*
- Write your wealth plan, legacy letters, or book
- Teach others how to fish—not just feed them

RELATIONSHIPS

- Raise, mentor, or guide people with emotional intelligence
- Don't just love—lead
- Refuse to settle, chase, or shrink
- Let every relationship in your life reflect who you've *become*—not who you were healing from

¤ **Final Thoughts:**

- Emotion is information, not instruction.
- Money is a magnifier, not a healer.
- Health is the engine. Love is the compass. Wealth is the vehicle.

If you master all three—calm becomes your default, purpose becomes your brand, and peace becomes your permanent address.

OTHER BOOKS BY TIERRE FORD

CONTROL THE PULSE

www.ingramcontent.com/pod-product-compliance
Lightning Source LLC
Chambersburg PA
CBHW050338010526
44119CB00049B/597